From the Bible-Teaching Ministry of
Charles R. Swindoll

Insight's Old Testament *Handbook*

A Practical Look at Each Book

INSIGHT'S OLD TESTAMENT HANDBOOK
A Practical Look at Each Book

From the Bible-Teaching Ministry of Charles R. Swindoll

Charles R. Swindoll has devoted his life to the clear, practical teaching and application of God's Word and His grace. A pastor at heart, Chuck has served as senior pastor to congregations in Texas, Massachusetts, and California. He currently pastors Stonebriar Community Church in Frisco, Texas, but Chuck's listening audience extends far beyond a local church body. As a leading program in Christian broadcasting, *Insight for Living* airs in major Christian radio markets around the world, reaching people groups in languages they can understand. Chuck's extensive writing ministry has also served the body of Christ worldwide and his leadership as president and now chancellor of Dallas Theological Seminary has helped prepare and equip a new generation for ministry. Chuck and Cynthia, his partner in life and ministry, have four grown children and ten grandchildren.

The text for *Insight's Old Testament Handbook: A Practical Look at Each Book* was written by John Adair, Th.M., Ph.D., Dallas Theological Seminary and Kelley Mathews, Th.M., Dallas Theological Seminary.

Original charts were from the following series:

God's Masterwork, Volume 1 Genesis through 2 Chronicles
Copyright © 1978, 1979, 1997 by Charles R. Swindoll, Inc.
God's Masterwork, Volume 2 Ezra through Daniel
Copyright © 1979, 1980, 1997 by Charles R. Swindoll, Inc.
God's Masterwork, Volume 3 Hosea through Malachi
Copyright © 1980, 1997 by Charles R. Swindoll, Inc.

Published by
IFL Publishing House
A Division of Insight for Living
Post Office Box 251007
Plano, Texas 75025-1007

Editor in Chief: Cynthia Swindoll, President, Insight for Living
Executive Vice President: Wayne Stiles, Th.M., D.Min., Dallas Theological Seminary
Theological Editor: Derrick G. Jeter, Th.M., Dallas Theological Seminary
Content Editor: Amy L. Snedaker, B.A. English, Rhodes College
Copy Editors: Jim Craft, M.A., English, Mississippi College
Cari Harris, B.A., Journalism, Grand Canyon University
Project Coordinator, Creative Ministries: Melanie Munnell, M.A., Humanities, The University of Texas at Dallas
Project Coordinator, Communications: Karen Berard, B.A., Mass Communications, Texas State University-San Marcos
Proofreader: Paula McCoy, B.A., English, Texas A&M University-Commerce
Cover Designer: Margaret Gulliford, B.A., Graphic Design, Taylor University
Production Artist: Nancy Gustine, B.F.A., Advertising Art, University of North Texas
Cover Image: Todd Bolen / BiblePlaces.com

ISBN: 978-1-57972-863-2
Printed in the United States of America

TABLE OF CONTENTS

THE MAJOR PROPHETS

THE MINOR PROPHETS

APPENDIXES

A NOTE FROM CHUCK SWINDOLL

The Old Testament sure gets a bad rap these days.

You've probably heard about the increasingly popular picture some people paint of our God based on His actions in the Old Testament. Some suggest that we should be ashamed of God's anger and wrath displayed there. They believe that God in the Old Testament doesn't measure up to the lofty standards of Jesus in the New Testament. And they complain that God seems too much like that crusty, ornery Clint Eastwood-style neighbor who stands ready to shoot a stranger for the smallest infraction.

But they've missed it. Those who think the Old Testament paints the portrait of an ugly, vengeful God haven't looked closely enough to discover the beauty of God's grace, mercy, and redemption dripping off many of those pages.

God wasn't an angry, volatile Creator suddenly transformed into a gentle and forgiving friend at the coming of Jesus. No, God is the same yesterday, today, and forever. The Old Testament prepares us for what comes in the New Testament. It gives us repeated glimpses of God's compassion and mercy right alongside His righteous anger and His justice. The Old Testament shows us God's rejection of sin but also His desire to redeem His creation and bring hope to a lost and floundering world. All these Old Testament themes find their ultimate fulfillment in the person of Jesus.

So don't believe the naysayers who want to drive a wedge between the Testaments. Understand, there's no difference in divine inspiration. You can open your Bible to any one of these thirty-nine books in the Old Testament, and you will come to sections equally as inspired as any portion of the New Testament, including the words of Jesus. In either Testament, we have reliable information. We don't have to wonder about the cynics who suggest that the God of the Old Testament is the fiery fancy of a few overactive imaginations. No, the Old Testament reveals God to us because it comes from God.

The book you hold in your hands, *Insights Old Testament Handbook: A Practical Look at Each Book*, was developed from the deep conviction that the Old Testament is both valuable and reliable. The handbook offers a clear and concise picture of each of the Old Testament's thirty-nine books. From some of the basics such as identifying the author and the setting of the book to highlighting the significant themes that make the book unique, each chapter will add to your appreciation of this too-often-neglected part of the Bible. This handbook will help you to see how each of the Old Testament books can make a difference in your life today.

So don't buy the painting the naysayers are selling. Instead, take a closer look at the picture of the Old Testament in this resource. I think you'll find that the Old Testament has a lot more to offer than the reputation that sometimes precedes it.

Charles R. Swindoll

WHY BOTHER WITH THE OLD TESTAMENT?

Imagine for a moment what the Old Testament would look like if a child had written it.

> In the big inning the score was zero, because there was nothing but God, darkness, and some gas. And God said, "Give me a light," and someone did. Then God hit a home run and made the world out of some stuff and split the Adam and made Eve. Adam and Eve were naked and weren't embarrassed because mirrors hadn't been invented yet. Then Adam and Eve talked to a snake and ate a bad apple, and God drove them in His Chevy Cherub out of the garden to live in the suburbs.

Perhaps if a child had written the Old Testament, more people would read it. In fact, it might make more sense! Let's be honest—much of the Old Testament is just downright difficult to understand. After all, what are we to make of so much information about temples, priests, animal sacrifices, and cooking goats in their mothers' milk? How does any of that apply to us today? And what deep, spiritual truth is anyone to learn from God commanding Jeremiah to bury his underwear (Jeremiah 13:1–7) or telling the Israelites to avoid trimming their beards (Leviticus 19:27) or matchmaking Hosea with a prostitute (Hosea 1:2)?

It's true; the Old Testament is ancient and seems far removed from modern life. Why should we bother reading it? Why should we take it seriously? These are common and understandable questions. And the typical responses are also common and understandable. One common objection says that because we are New Testament Christians, the Old Testament doesn't apply to us. If it wasn't written to us in the first place, then why should we read it? Therefore, many people simply ignore its thirty-nine books altogether (or they ignore everything except Psalms and Proverbs because those are the Old Testament books attached to their New Testament pocket Bibles).

Perhaps worse than ignoring the Old Testament completely is the too common practice of cherry-picking our way through the Old Testament—finding verses we like here and there as if they were foods we choose in a buffet line. This method of reading the Old Testament refuses to recognize that these verses are part of a rich context and typically require some effort in order to discover the actual meaning of the text and apply it correctly.

Three Reasons Why We Should Read the Old Testament

Neither ignoring the Old Testament nor cherry-picking verses out of context is a recommended practice. In fact, most of us know deep down that we should read the Old Testament—all of it! But if we're honest, we must admit that we don't always follow that conviction with action. So why should we read the Old Testament? Three good answers tell us why.

Reason One: The New Testament Is Not Enough

It may sound like a startling statement, but the reality is that the New Testament alone simply does not tell us everything about God that He wants us to know. If we believe that the entire Bible comes from God (2 Timothy 3:16), then it stands to reason that God revealed Himself in the Old Testament for a purpose. In the Old Testament, we see God relate to a wide variety of people over thousands of years. These relationships reveal God's unmistakable consistency, His care for the little things of life, the results of His anger over sin, and His desire to redeem human beings in spite of our rebellion. God's character and nature shine through in strikingly accessible ways throughout the Old Testament, if only we'd dig a little deeper into it.

Reason Two: Its People Reveal the Struggle and Blessing of Living with God

One thing the Old Testament has in spades is people. From Adam, Cain, and Noah to Moses, David, and Esther, we find in the Old Testament individuals of all kinds, at various levels of maturity, and at different places in their walks with God. Some followed Him. Others fell away. It's in the stories of these people that we see the life of faith lived out or cast aside. It's in these lives that the real difficulty of following after God becomes clear. By deriving timeless principles from the lives of the Old Testament, we can learn from the failures of these unique men and women, derive comfort from their frustrations and struggles, and gain inspiration from their faithfulness.

Reason Three: It's the Bible Jesus Read

When the Son of God walked the earth, the New Testament had not yet been written. Jesus's access to teaching about God? The Old Testament. It was the first and primary place He turned to, because the Jewish people had no other Scriptures. The thirty-nine books of the Old Testament shined brightly in Jesus's Jewish community, pointing the way to the truth, both about the Father . . . and ultimately about Jesus Himself. Jesus quoted the Old Testament when confronting the Pharisees about the greatest commandment of the Law (Matthew 22:34–39). He even highlighted the importance of the Old Testament in a conversation with a couple of His disciples. Jesus explained to these men how the entire Old Testament—from the books of Moses to the books of the prophets—taught about Him, the long-awaited Messiah (Luke 24:27). If the Old Testament was so important to Jesus and to the disciples, shouldn't we, too, mine its depths for the riches within?

How to Use this Handbook

When reading most books, you simply pick up the book and start with page 1. You can do that with this one, of course, but *Insight's Old Testament Handbook* is a little different. It is designed to be used as a resource as you study your Bible. As you read the Old Testament, bring along this handbook. From information on authors and settings to summaries, themes, and charts, the information contained in this handbook will provide a helpful context for what you read in the Old Testament. We hope you will find this resource to be a valuable addition to your ongoing study of God's Word.

INSIGHT'S OLD TESTAMENT *Handbook*

THE PENTATEUCH

Derived from a Greek word that means "five books," the Pentateuch is a common name for the first five books of the Old Testament: Genesis, Exodus, Leviticus, Numbers, and Deuteronomy. These books were each written by Moses and chronicle God's creation of the world; God's choice to draw humanity to Himself through the people of Israel; Moses's delivery of the Law to the people; and God's leading the Israelites out of slavery, through the wilderness, and to the edge of their Promised Land.

GENESIS

Who Wrote the Book?

Old Testament books seldom include a byline. So we look to outside sources to discover authorship. Jewish tradition and other biblical authors name Moses, the prophet and deliverer of Israel, as the author of the entire Pentateuch—the first five books of the Old Testament. His education in the courts of Egypt (Acts 7:22) and his close communion with Yahweh—the Hebrew name for God—support this premise. Jesus Himself confirmed Moses's authorship (John 5:45–47), as did the scribes and Pharisees of His time (Matthew 19:7; 22:24).

From the Hebrew word *toledoth*, the first book of the Bible is titled "Genesis" in the Septuagint, the Greek translation of the Jewish Scriptures (see Appendix D). The word means "beginning, origin,"[1] or generation and is a foundational theme that winds throughout the book.

Moses wrote Genesis for the people of Israel, whom he led out of slavery in Egypt back to the land of their forefathers. Genesis provides a history of those forefathers—their origins, their journeys, and their covenants with God. Because the events contained in the rest of the Pentateuch are responses to the promises of God found in Genesis, such a history of God's interaction with their ancestors would have provided encouragement and inspiration to the former slaves seeking freedom and prosperity in the Promised Land.

Where Are We?

The first eleven chapters of Genesis paint the early history of the human race in broad strokes. After the great flood, the focus narrows to God's dealings with one family living in Mesopotamia, a family headed by

Abram, later called Abraham. From the Euphrates River (in modern-day Iraq) over to what is now Syria, events move south into Canaan (modern-day Israel) and Egypt. (See Map of the Pentateuch, Part One in Appendix A for a helpful visual reference to important places referred to in Genesis.)

Genesis covers the most extensive period of time in all of Scripture, longer than the other books in the Bible combined! While the ancient history recounted in the first eleven chapters gives no indication of time span, Abram's story begins around 2091 BC (Genesis 12:1), and the book ends with Joseph's death in Egypt around 1805 BC (50:26).

Why Is Genesis so Important?

To the original readers of Genesis, the book was valued as a history of their people. It told them the story of how God created the world and dealt with all humanity until He initiated a personal relationship with their forefather Abraham. Genesis revealed to them the eternal promises God made to Abraham, Isaac, and Jacob—promises which extended to their descendants. It provided comfort and hope for the downtrodden Hebrews as they waited to return to their "promised land."

For later readers, Genesis offers a thorough background to the rest of the Bible. Here we learn ancient history and geography and are introduced to significant people and events found later in the Bible. God also reveals many facets of His nature through His dealings with people. We learn of the origin of sin, of its destructive effect on humanity, and of God's plan to atone for that sin through a future Son of the people of Israel (Genesis 3:15; 22:18; 49:10).

What's the Big Idea?

The Bible is divided into two major parts, the Old and New Testaments. *Testament* is another word for *covenant*. Covenants figure prominently into the story of Genesis, for they help define God's relationship with His people at various times. Sin broke the perfect peace between God and humanity (Genesis 3) and instead of enjoying the blessing God intended, humanity was burdened with the curse. But God established His plan for redemption and blessing through covenants, first with Abraham (Genesis 12:1–5), reaffirmed with Isaac (26:1–35), then with Jacob (28:1–22). These promises applied to the Israelites in Egypt and to later generations. Genesis sets the stage for the rest of God's plan to redeem the world through His Son, Jesus Christ.

How Do I Apply This?

It's easy to get lost in the genealogies and accounts in Genesis without seeing the big picture. Keep God, not just the people, in mind as you read through the book. Consider His character qualities. If you were an Israelite just released from slavery and reading this for the first time, would you marvel at God's power over creation? Or His anger over sin? Or the way He fulfilled His promises to everyone? Awareness of each of these characteristics should evoke worship . . . and hope. Remember that the Lord is strong, faithful, and just. And His desire to bless His creation will one day be fully realized.

Genesis

	Creation *CHAPTERS 1–2*	Fall *CHAPTERS 3–5*	Flood *CHAPTERS 6–9*	Nations *CHAPTERS 10–11*	Abraham *CHAPTERS 12–25*	Isaac *CHAPTERS 26–27*	Jacob *CHAPTERS 28–36*	Joseph *CHAPTERS 37–50*
Beginnings	Beginning of the human race				Beginning of the chosen race			
Result	Confusion and scattering				Bondage in Egypt			
History	Primeval history				Patriarchal history			
Chronology	Over 2,000 years				Approximately 300 years			
Emphasis	Four major events				Four important people			
Key Words and Phrases	"In the beginning" (1:1) "Generations" (5:1; 6:9; 10:1; 11:10; 11:27; 25:12; 25:19; 36:1; 37:2)							
Theme	God promises to redeem and bless His people.							
Key Verses	3:15; 12:3							
Christ in Genesis	Pictured in the seed of the woman (3:15); Melchizedek, the high priest (14:18); the humiliation and exaltation of Joseph (chapters 37–50)							

EXODUS

Who Wrote the Book?

As with Genesis, early Jewish traditions name Moses as the most likely and best qualified person to have authored Exodus. This theory is supported by a number of factors. Moses's unique education in the royal courts of Egypt certainly provided him the opportunity and ability to pen these works (Acts 7:22). Internal evidence (material found within the text of Exodus itself) adds support for Moses's authorship. Many conversations, events, and geographical details could be known only by an eyewitness or participant. For example, the text reads: "Moses then wrote down everything the LORD had said," (Exodus 24:4 NIV). Additionally, other biblical books refer to "the law of Moses" (Joshua 1:7; 1 Kings 2:3), indicating that Exodus, which includes rules and regulations, was written by Moses. Jesus Himself introduced a quote from Exodus 20:12 and 21:17 with the words, "For Moses said" (Mark 7:10), confirming His own understanding of the book's author.

The title "Exodus" comes from the Septuagint (see Appendix D), which derived it from the primary event found in the book, the deliverance from slavery and "exodus" or departure of the Israelite nation out of Egypt by the hand of Yahweh, the God of their forefathers.

Where Are We?

Exodus begins in the Egyptian region called Goshen. The people then traveled out of Egypt and, it is traditionally believed, moved toward the southern end of the Sinai Peninsula. They camped at Mount Sinai, where Moses received God's commandments. (See Map of the Pentateuch, Part Two in Appendix A to see the route of the Israelites from Egypt to Mount Sinai.)

The book covers a period of approximately eighty years, from shortly before Moses's birth (c. 1526 BC) to the events that occurred at Mount Sinai in 1446 BC.

Why Is Exodus so Important?

In Exodus we witness God beginning to fulfill His promises to Abraham, Isaac, and Jacob. Though the children of Israel were enslaved in a foreign land, God miraculously and dramatically delivered them to freedom. He then established Israel as a theocratic nation under His covenant with Moses on Mount Sinai. The ten plagues, the Passover, the parting of the Red Sea, the fearsome majesty of God's presence at Mount Sinai, the giving of the Ten Commandments, the building of the tabernacle . . . these events from Exodus are foundational to the Jewish faith. And they provide crucial background context to help future readers of Scripture understand the entire Bible's message of redemption. The frequency of references to Exodus by various biblical writers, and even Jesus's own words, testify to its importance.

What's the Big Idea?

The overall theme of Exodus is redemption—how God delivered the Israelites and made them His special people. After He rescued them from slavery, God provided the Law, which gave instructions on how the people could be consecrated or made holy. He established a system of sacrifice, which guided them in appropriate worship behavior. Just as significantly, God provided detailed directions on the building of His tabernacle, or tent. He intended to live among the Israelites and manifest His *shekinah* glory (Exodus 40:34–35)—another proof that they were indeed His people.

The Mosaic Covenant, unveiled initially through the Decalogue (Ten Commandments), provides the foundation for the beliefs and practices of Judaism, from common eating practices to complex worship regulations. Through the Law, God says that all of life relates to God. Nothing is outside His jurisdiction.

How Do I Apply This?

Like the Israelites who left Egypt, all believers in Christ are redeemed and consecrated to God. Under the Mosaic Covenant, people annually sacrificed unblemished animals according to specific regulations in order to have their sins covered, or borne, by that animal. The author of the New Testament book of Hebrews tells us, "But those sacrifices are an annual reminder of sins, because it is impossible for the blood of bulls and goats to take away sins" (Hebrews 10:3–4 NIV). Jesus's sacrifice on the cross fulfilled the Law. As the perfect Lamb of God, He took away our sin permanently when He sacrificed Himself on our behalf. "We have been made holy through the sacrifice of the body of Jesus Christ once for all" (10:10 NIV).

Have you accepted His sacrifice on your behalf? Are you truly "redeemed"? If you'd like to learn about this, see "How to Begin a Relationship with God" in the back of this book.

EXODUS

GENESIS — 350 Years — Groan of the Israelites	Bondage	Deliverance	Journey	Law	Tabernacle	Glory of the Lord
	Israelites became numerous New Pharaoh Plan to destroy Israelites Moses	Blood, Frogs, Gnats, Flies, Livestock, Boils, Hail, Locusts, Darkness, Death Passover Exodus	Cloud and fire Red Sea Grumbling	Moral Civil Social	Outer court 150 feet x 75 feet Inner court 45 feet x 15 feet	
	CHAPTERS 1–2	*CHAPTERS 3–12*	*CHAPTERS 13–18*	*CHAPTERS 19–24*	*CHAPTERS 25–40*	
Location	Egypt		En route	Mount Sinai		
Time	430 years		3 months	1 year		
Theme	Suffering and liberation of people of God		Guidance of God	Worship of God		
Key Verses	6:6; 12:40–42; 19:5–6					
Christ in Exodus	Passover lamb (chapter 12); sacrificial offering, tabernacle, articles of worship (chapters 25–40); His leadership and deliverance are pictured in Moses; His purity and intercession are pictured in the high priest.					

LEVITICUS

Who Wrote the Book?

The content of Leviticus relates directly to Exodus, providing evidence that the same hand penned both books. The arguments that support Moses's writing of Exodus also uphold Moses's authorship of Leviticus (see the previous chapter). Additionally, we find more than fifty occasions when the text says something like, "The LORD spoke to Moses" (Leviticus 1:1; 4:1; 5:14; 6:1). The New Testament also refers to Moses as the author of passages from Leviticus (Matthew 8:4; Luke 2:22; Hebrews 8:5).

The word *Leviticus* derives from the tribe of Levi, whose members were set aside by the Lord to be His priests and worship leaders. As a title, the word is translated from the Septuagint, meaning "'pertaining to the Levites,' and although that tribe as such is not emphasized throughout the book, the priestly subject matter renders the title appropriate."[1] Its content was originally meant to instruct the new nation of Israel in proper worship and right living, so that they might reflect the character of their divine King.

Where Are We?

The Law found in Leviticus was spoken by God to Moses at or near Mount Sinai, where the Israelites camped for some time. Because God delivered these detailed laws after the original Ten Commandments, the most probable date for their revelation is 1446 BC. Whether every law was written down at that time is impossible to determine; it may be that they were codified progressively during the ensuing forty-year wandering.

Why Is Leviticus so Important?

"The book of Leviticus was the first book studied by a Jewish child; yet is often among the last books of the Bible to be studied by a Christian."[2] Today's readers are often put off by the book's lists of laws regarding diet, sacrifice, and social behavior. But within these highly detailed directives we discover the holiness—the separateness, distinction, and utter "otherness"—of God. And we learn how sin devastates humanity's relationship with their Creator.

God established the sacrificial system so that His covenant people might enjoy His fellowship through worship; it also allowed for repentance and renewal:

> When an Israelite worshiper laid his hand on the animal victim, he identified himself with the animal as his substitute . . . this accomplished a symbolic transfer of his sin and a legal transfer of his guilt to the animal victim. God then accepted the slaughter of the animal . . . as a ransom payment for the particular sin which occasioned it.[3]

Many years after Moses wrote Leviticus, Jesus came to offer Himself as the ultimate sacrifice, holy and perfect, once for all, fulfilling the Law and rendering future animal sacrifices unnecessary and void (Hebrews 10:10).

What's the Big Idea?

The overall message of Leviticus is sanctification. The book communicates that receiving God's forgiveness and acceptance should be followed by holy living and spiritual growth. Now that Israel had been redeemed by God, they were to be purified into a people worthy of their God. "You shall be holy, for I the Lord your God am holy," says Leviticus 19:2. In Leviticus we learn that God loves to be approached, but we must do so on His terms.

How Do I Apply This?

This theme of holiness extends to the church. In the New Testament, 1 Peter 1:15–16 references Leviticus 19:2 when it says: "like the Holy One who called you, be holy yourselves also in all your behavior; because it is written, 'You shall be holy, for I am holy.'" Those who are redeemed by the mercies of God offer different sacrifices today; they offer themselves (Romans 12:1).

Like He did with the Israelites, God has redeemed and consecrated Christians. Jesus offered Himself as the perfect sacrifice on our behalf, taking the punishment that we deserved so that we might be forgiven. Those who place their trust in Jesus's atoning act become God's children, saved by grace (Ephesians 2:8–9).

If you are His child, then He wants you to reflect His character. He is sanctifying you much like He did the nation of Israel. Does your life echo His? In what ways are you growing more like Christ?

Leviticus

	The Way to God *Access*	The Walk with God *Lifestyle*
	The approach: offerings The representative: priest The laws: cleansing *Physically* *Spiritually*	Practical guidelines Chronological observances Severe consequences Verbal promises
	CHAPTERS 1–17	*CHAPTERS 18–27*
Emphasis	Ritual (for worship)	Practical (for living)
Location	Mount Sinai . . . one full year	
Key Word	"Holy" (appears 90 times)	
Theme	How sinful humanity should worship a holy God	
Key Verses	17:11; 19:2; 20:7–8	
Christ in Leviticus	Pictured in each sacrifice and ritual	

NUMBERS

Who Wrote the Book?

As it does for the rest of the Pentateuch, universal Jewish and Christian tradition attributes the authorship of the book of Numbers to Moses. Moses is the central figure within the book, and in at least two instances Numbers mentions him recording events by the Lord's commands (Numbers 33:2; 36:13).

The name "Numbers" is a translation of *Arithmoi*, from the Septuagint (see Appendix D), titled thus because the book contains many statistics, population counts, tribal and priestly figures, and other numerical data. The Hebrew name comes from the first sentence of the book and means "in the desert of"; it is perhaps an even more accurate description of the book's content, which follows the Israelites through almost forty years of wandering in the desert.[1]

Where Are We?

The events of the book began in the second year after the Israelites departed Egypt, as they camped at Mount Sinai around 1444 BC (Numbers 1:1). The narrative ends thirty-eight years later "in the plains of Moab by the Jordan opposite Jericho" (36:13) in 1406 BC. Numbers records the people's long wandering in the desert of Sinai, their time at the oasis of Kadesh-barnea, and their eventual arrival at the banks of the Jordan River across from the Promised Land. (See Map of the Pentateuch, Part Two in Appendix A for a visual reference to these journeys.)

The Lord directed the message of Numbers toward the younger generation, children of the former slaves who escaped through the Red Sea. Except for Joshua, Caleb, and Moses, the older generation—everyone twenty years old or older at the time of the first census—died before the completion of Numbers, due to their disobedience and disbelief (Numbers 14:22–30). Moses completed the book before his death (Deuteronomy 31:24).

Why Is Numbers so Important?

Numbers takes the reader on a long and winding path through a desert of excruciating detail. The book records census results for all twelve tribes not once, but twice; it documents priestly instructions for handling the Ark of the Covenant and the tabernacle; and it even spells out the placement of the tribes when they camped. But through it all, we cannot doubt God's unfailing direction over the nation.

As a history of the nation not yet established in the land promised them long ago, this book unveils significant events sometimes referenced later in Scripture. Joshua and Caleb alone among the twelve spies encouraged Israel to take possession of the land (Numbers 13–14; Joshua 14:7); Moses struck a rock and water spouted forth (Numbers 20:11; Psalm 106:32); Moses lifted up a bronze serpent on a pole so that believing Israelites might be healed of their snake bites (Numbers 21:6–9; John 3:14); and Balaam was rebuked by his donkey (Numbers 22:21–34; Revelation 2:14).

What's the Big Idea?

In this book, the people of Israel tested God's patience, and He in turn tested their endurance and faithfulness. Though the people failed many times, God showed His own faithfulness by His constant presence leading the way: through a cloud by day and a pillar of fire by night.

More than just a history lesson, the book of Numbers reveals how God reminded Israel that He does not tolerate rebellion, complaining, and disbelief without invoking consequences. He taught His people how to walk with Him—not just with their feet through the wilderness but with their mouths in worship, hands in service, and lives as witnesses to the surrounding nations. He was their God, they were His people, and He expected them to act like it.

How Do I Apply This?

Modern readers can take away from Numbers not only a thorough history of Israel's early days but also a renewed sense of God's delight in obedience. He is our God, too, and He wants us to live righteously, worshipping Him through our words and works.

The journey of the Israelites through the wilderness earned the apostle Paul's notice when he penned his first letter to the Corinthian church. "These things happened," he wrote in 1 Corinthians 10:6, "as examples for us, so that we would not crave evil things as they also craved."

Do you see any resemblance between the grumbling, rebellious Israelites and yourself? How can you avoid following their example? With humility and sincerity, pray for a soft heart, open to God's guiding hand.

NUMBERS

	Preparation	Pessimism	Punishment
	Census Organization Sanctification	Complaining Doubting Promised Land rejected	Wandering Old generation dies New census
	CHAPTERS 1–9	*CHAPTERS 10–14*	*CHAPTERS 15–36*
Location	Mount Sinai	En route to Kadesh-barnea	Wilderness wandering
Time	20 days	Several months	38 years
Key Word	Wilderness		
Theme	The price of disbelief and disobedience		
Key Verses	14:22–23		
Christ in Numbers	Pictured in manna (compare John 6:31–33); water from rock (compare 1 Corinthians 10:4); bronze serpent (compare John 3:14); in Balaam's prophecy (Numbers 24:17); pillar of cloud and of fire; cities of refuge		

DEUTERONOMY

Who Wrote the Book?

Deuteronomy means "second law," a term mistakenly derived from the Hebrew word *mishneh* in Deuteronomy 17:18. In that context, Moses simply commands the king to make a "copy of the law."[1] But Deuteronomy does something more than give a simple copy of the Law. The book offers a restatement of the Law for a new generation, rather than a mere copy of what had gone before. Deuteronomy records this "second law"—namely Moses's series of sermons in which he restated God's commands originally given to the Israelites some forty years earlier in Exodus and Leviticus.

"These are the words which Moses spoke to all Israel," says Deuteronomy 1:1. Mosaic authorship of this book finds the usual support from Jewish tradition (with the entire Pentateuch) but also from within the biblical text. Several times, Deuteronomy asserts Moses as author (1:1; 4:44; 29:1). Speaking to Joshua, Moses's successor, the Lord referred to this "book of the law" as that which Moses commanded (Joshua 1:8). And when future Old Testament and New Testament writers quoted from Deuteronomy, they often referred to it as originating with Moses (1 Kings 2:3; 2 Kings 14:6; Ezra 3:2; Nehemiah 1:7; Malachi 4:4; Matthew 19:7; Luke 20:28).

Some obvious editorial changes were made to the text sometime after Moses recorded the bulk of it. For instance, he could not have written the final chapter, which dealt with his death. However, these and other small changes do not affect the generally accepted authorship of Moses.

Where Are We?

Deuteronomy was written around 1406 BC, at the end of the forty years of wandering endured by the nation of Israel. At the time, the people were camped on the east side of the Jordan River, on the plains of Moab, across from the city of Jericho (Deuteronomy 1:1; 29:1). They were on the verge of entering the land that had been promised centuries earlier to their forefathers (Genesis 12:1, 6–9). The children who had left Egypt were now adults, ready to conquer and settle the Promised Land. Before that could happen, the Lord reiterated through Moses His covenant with them.

Why Is Deuteronomy so Important?

Moses addressed his words to "all Israel" at least twelve times. This phrase emphasized the nation's unity, initiated by their covenant with God at Mount Sinai and forged in the wilderness. In the midst of widespread polytheism, Israel was distinctive in that they worshipped one God, Yahweh. Their God was totally unique; there was none other like Him among all the "gods" of the nations surrounding them. Deuteronomy 6:4 codifies this belief in the *Shema*, the basic confession of faith in Judaism even today. "Hear, O Israel! The Lord [Yahweh] is our God, the Lord [Yahweh] is one!"

Deuteronomy also restates the Ten Commandments and many other laws given in Exodus and Leviticus. The book delivered to Israel God's instructions on how to live a blessed life in the Promised Land. Chapters 27 and 28 specify the blessings of obedience and the curses of disobedience.

What's the Big Idea?

Unlike the unconditional covenant God made with Abraham, the covenant between Yahweh and Israel was bilateral—a two-way street. God would keep His promise to bless the nation if the people remained faithful. The adult Israelites were too young to have participated in the first covenant ceremony at Mount Sinai. Therefore, Moses reviewed the Law at the doorstep to the Promised Land, urging this new generation to re-covenant with Yahweh, to recommit themselves to His ways.

How Do I Apply This?

In Moses's conclusion, he entreated the people,

> "I have set before you life and death, the blessing and the curse. So choose life in order that you may live, you and your descendants, by loving the LORD your God, by obeying His voice, and by holding fast to Him; for this is your life and the length of your days."
> (Deuteronomy 30:19–20)

"This" in verse 20 refers to loving the Lord your God, obeying, and holding fast to Him. *That* is life! Our relationship with God is to be marked by faithfulness, loyalty, love, and devotion. Think of an ideal marriage—that's the picture of how God wants us to cling to Him (Ephesians 5:28–32).

How closely do you cling to God? Pray and recommit your heart to that all-important relationship with Him.

DEUTERONOMY

WILDERNESS WANDERING	Looking Back	Looking Up	Looking Ahead
	REMEMBER!	REMEMBER!	REMEMBER!
	Failure at Kadesh-barnea	Blessings accompany obedience	The land is yours; possess it!
	Faithfulness of God	Compromises weaken distinctives	The Lord is holy; obey Him!
		Consequences follow disobedience	
	CHAPTERS 1–4	*CHAPTERS 5–26*	*CHAPTERS 27–34*
Location	Everything occurs on the edge of the Promised Land of Canaan.		
Leadership	At the beginning of the book, MOSES is the leader (34:5) . . .		. . . by the end of the book, JOSHUA is the leader (1:38; 34:9)
Time	The sermons recorded in Deuteronomy were first spoken (1:6) then written (31:24) during a period of 40 days (compare Deuteronomy 1:3; 34:8; Joshua 4:19).		
Theme	Remember to love the Lord your God and keep His commandments.		
Key Verses	6:4–9; 10:12–13; 30:19–20		
Christ in Deuteronomy	"The LORD your God will raise up for you a prophet like me from among you, from your countrymen, you shall listen to him" (18:15); Moses himself is also a type of Christ.		

THE HISTORICAL BOOKS

We know the next twelve books of the Old Testament as the Historical books. Joshua through Esther covers nearly a thousand years of Israelite history. Beginning with Israel's entrance into the land of Canaan under the direction of Joshua, these books highlight Israel's initial capture of the land; the ups and downs of life during the rules of judges and kings; the tragic exiles of the northern and southern kingdoms; and with Ezra through Esther, the glorious return from exile to the land of Israel.

JOSHUA

Who Wrote the Book?

The book's primary figure gives it its title. *Joshua* means "Yahweh saves,"[1] an appropriate name for the man who led Israel, under God's command, to victorious conquest of the Promised Land. Scholars believe that Joshua himself or a scribe under his direction penned most of the book. Early chapters include firsthand experiences (the NIV uses the pronouns "we" and "us" in Joshua 5:1, 6, for example) and military details worthy of being known and recorded by a general. Joshua 24:26 refers to Joshua writing a portion of the book himself. After Joshua's death, the high priests Eleazar or Phinehas may have supplemented some material in this book that alludes to events after the conquest (15:13–19; 19:47; 24:29–33).[2]

Where Are We?

The events of the book of Joshua span about twenty-five years, starting soon after the death of Moses (Joshua 1:1) around 1406 BC, before the conquest commenced. The conquest of Canaan took about seven years, and Joshua's final address and subsequent death came almost twenty years later. The book begins with the nation of Israel poised at the banks of the Jordan River, across from Jericho. It records the details of numerous military campaigns that defeated the inhabitants of the land. The book ends with Joshua's regathering of the nation for his final exhortation.

This history was written to the victorious Israelites who had settled the land. Though they were newly established as conquerors, Joshua reminded them that the conquest was incomplete: "very much of the land remains to be possessed" (13:1).

Why Is Joshua so Important?

The book of Joshua records the culmination of Israel's journey to the Promised Land. Here we see God fulfill His promise to give the land of Canaan to Jacob's descendants. Joshua portrays the Lord as their general, the One who would lead His people in victorious battle if they would trust and obey.

Joshua recounted a story of contradictions. On the one hand, God gave the land that He had promised to the nation. On the other hand, the people failed to possess the land completely, allowing some inhabitants to remain. God fulfilled His side of the bargain, but the Israelites did not finish the job. The Canaanite peoples became a damaging influence on Israel as years went by.

In this book we find accounts of faithfulness: Rahab the harlot (Joshua 2:1–21), the battle of Jericho (6:1–27), and Caleb the warrior (14:6–14). We also witness disobedience and its consequences: Achan's sin (7:1) and the resulting loss at Ai (7:5), failure of some tribes to annihilate the enemy as God commanded, and even Joshua making a treaty with the Gibeonites without first seeking the Lord (9:1–27).

What's the Big Idea?

The book of Joshua was written to the descendants of those who conquered the land, as a historical account of how they had come to settle there. It celebrates God as general, defender, and king. It shows the geographical boundaries given to each tribe of Israel. Even more significantly, the book of Joshua serves as the connecting narrative between the days of Moses and the days of the judges, during which the book was first circulated. That which Moses began and endured in the wilderness, Joshua was able to claim victoriously in the land. God's promises through the ages were being fulfilled before the people's eyes. "Not one of the good promises which the Lord had made to the house of Israel failed; all came to pass" (Joshua 21:45).

How Do I Apply This?

The last few verses of Joshua narrate three burials: Joshua (Joshua 24:29–30), the bones of Joseph (24:32), and Eleazar the high priest (24:33). Strange as it may seem, these burials proclaim God's character. All three men were associated with Israel's days in captivity (Joseph long ago when Jacob's family first settled in Egypt, and Joshua and Eleazar as young men on the long journey through the wilderness). And now all three lay at rest in the land of promise, witnesses to God's faithfulness.

God is the ultimate promise-keeper. As faithful and present as He was with Israel, so He is with us. "Be strong and courageous! Do not tremble or be dismayed, for the LORD your God is with you wherever you go" (1:9).

JOSHUA

OUTSIDE CANAAN / PROMISES GIVEN

Commissioning the Leader Preparing the People	Conquering the Enemy		Dividing the Spoil				Warning the Victors
Invasion of land	Subjection of land		Distribution of land				The Conclusion
	CENTRAL CAMPAIGN		PHASE ONE	PHASE TWO	PHASE THREE		
The commission (1) The spying (2) The Jordan (3) The memorials (4) The consecration (5)	Jericho (6) Defeat at Ai (7) Victory at Ai (8) Gibeonites (9)	Southern Campaign (10) Northern campaign and survey (11) Summary by kings (12)	Rueben, Gad, ½ Manasseh (13) Caleb's auto-biography (14) Judah (15) Ephraim (16) ½ Manasseh (17)	Benjamín (18) Simeon, Zebulun, Issachar, Asher, Naphtali, Dan, Joshua (19)	Cities of refuge (20) Levites — 48 towns (21)	Civil war threat (22)	Separation (23) Service (24)
CHAPTERS 1–5	*CHAPTERS 6–9*	*CHAPTERS 10–12*	*CHAPTERS 13–17*	*CHAPTERS 18–19*	*CHAPTERS 20–21*	*CHAPTERS 22*	*CHAPTERS 23–24*

INSIDE CANAAN / PROMISES FULFILLED

Theme	Obedient faith brings abundant blessing.
Key Verses	1:8; 24:14–15
Christ in Joshua	Typified by Joshua, a victorious leader whose name means "Yahweh is salvation"; pictured in Rahab's scarlet cord, which symbolizes safety through Christ's blood

JUDGES

Who Wrote the Book?

The text of Judges gives no indication as to who wrote the book, but Jewish tradition names the prophet Samuel as the author. The namesake of 1 and 2 Samuel, Samuel was the last of the judges, one of the special leaders whom God raised up during this time period to rescue His people. The judges did not oversee merely legal matters, as in our sense of the role; their tasks often included military and administrative authority as well.

Why Samuel? The author of Judges certainly lived in the early days of the monarchy. The recurring statement, "in those days there was no king in Israel" (Judges 17:6; 18:1; 19:1; 21:25), points out a contrast between the events happening in the book and the time of its writing. Clues within Judges suggest it was written before David established his throne in Jerusalem (1004 BC), yet after Saul was anointed king (1051 BC) (compare Judges 1:21 with 2 Samuel 5:6–7 and Judges 1:29 with 1 Kings 9:16). Also, Samuel was known to write on occasion (1 Samuel 10:25).

Where Are We?

We think about the judges as both a period of time and a book of the Bible. The period of the judges began after the death of Joshua in the early fourteenth century BC (Joshua 24:29) and continued until Saul was crowned king of Israel by the prophet Samuel in 1051 BC (1 Samuel 10:24). The book of Judges acts as the sequel to the book of Joshua, linked by comparable accounts of Joshua's death (Joshua 24:29–31; Judges 2:6–9). Events within the book of Judges span the geographical breadth of the nation, happening in a variety of cities, towns, and battlefields. Scholars believe some of the judges ruled simultaneously in separate geographical regions. Attempts to calculate the exact amount of time covered in Judges are inconclusive, but generally, the book begins soon after the death of Joshua and ends in the years just before the entrance of Samuel onto the scene, a period of about three hundred years.

The contents of Judges were likely not written chronologically. The final few chapters (Judges 17–21) give an overview of the moral climate during those days and, rather than occurring after the period of the judges listed earlier in the book, they probably happened in and around the times of various judges mentioned in earlier chapters.

Why Is Judges so Important?

The time of the judges brought about great apostasy in Israel. The nation underwent political and religious turmoil as the people tried to possess those parts of the land that had not yet been fully conquered. The tribes fought among themselves, as well, nearly wiping out the tribes of Manasseh (Judges 12) and Benjamin (20–21). The pattern of behavior in the book of Judges is clear: the people rebelled through idolatry and disbelief, God brought judgment through foreign oppression, God raised up a deliverer—or judge, and the people repented and turned back to God. When the people fell back into sin, the cycle started over again.

Ironically, in this book we meet many heroes of faith: Othniel, Gideon, Samson, Shamgar, Deborah, Jephthah, Ehud . . . flawed individuals who answered God's call to deliver the Israelites in sometimes dramatic form. The book includes many of the most graphic, violent, and disturbing scenes in all Scripture—some in the name of righteousness, others in the name of evil.

What's the Big Idea?

The primary message of Judges is that God will not allow sin to go unpunished. As Exodus established, Israel was God's people—He was their King. They had forsaken the covenant established at Mount Sinai. In Judges, He disciplined them for following other gods, disobeying

His sacrificial laws, engaging in blatant immorality, and descending into anarchy at times. Yet because they were His people, He listened to their cries for mercy and raised up leaders to deliver them. Unfortunately, even these godly individuals did not wield sufficient influence to change the nation's direction. The people's inability to resist sinful Canaanite influences eventually revealed their desire for a centralized monarchy, led by a righteous king whom God would choose as His intermediary.

How Do I Apply This?

Memory is a gift. Remembering the past teaches us countless lessons about how to live today. The Israelites forgot. They did not remember the miraculous events that brought them to their land or the covenant that united them to their God. But God did not forget His covenant—and because of His great love for His people, He disciplined His sinful children so that they might return to Him.

Have you forgotten the great works God has done in your life? Perhaps your difficult circumstances are overpowering your faith. Do you feel as if He is disciplining you right now? Know that He disciplines those He loves (Hebrews 12:5–11). Return to Him. Remember, trust, and obey. He is waiting with open arms.

JUDGES

JOSHUA ca. 1375 BC — SAMUEL ca. 1075 BC

	Causes of Failure	Course of Failure	Curses from Failure
	Incomplete obedience (1:1–2:5) Idolatry (2:6–3:4) Intermarriage 3:5–6	MESOPOTAMIA 8 years OTHNIEL (3:9–11) MOABITES 18 years EHUD (3:15–30) SHAMGAR (3:31) CANAAN 20 years DEBORAH BARAK (4:4–5:31) MIDIANITES 7 years GIDEON (6:11–8:28) ABIMELECH 3 years TOLA JAIR (10:1–5) AMMONITES 18 years JEPHTHAH (11:1–12:7) IBZAN (12:8–10) ELON (12:11–12) ABDON (12:13–15) PHILISTINES 40 years SAMSON (13:2–16:31)	Idolatry Immorality Anarchy
	Defeat (1) Review (2)	Cycles of Misery Disobedience Bondage Misery Liberation and Rest Compromises	Micah (family) (17) Danites (tribe) (18) Levite and concubine (19) Civil war (20) Mourning (21)
	CHAPTERS 1–2	*CHAPTERS 3–16*	*CHAPTERS 17–21*
	DEFEAT	DISOBEDIENCE	DISGRACE
Theme	Compromise brings failure.		
Key Verses	17:6; 21:25		
Christ in Judges	Prefigured as the ultimate judge and deliverer		

RUTH

Who Wrote the Book?

According to the Talmud (Jewish tradition), the prophet Samuel wrote the book of Ruth. The text itself says nothing of the author, but whoever wrote it was a skilled storyteller. It has been called the most beautiful short story ever written.

The final words of the book link Ruth with her great-grandson, David (Ruth 4:17–22), so we know it was written after his anointing. The genealogy at the end of the book shows David's lineage through the days of the judges, acting as a support for his rightful kingship. Solomon is not mentioned, leading some to believe the book was written before David ascended the throne.

Where Are We?

The events of Ruth occurred sometime between 1160 BC and 1100 BC, during the latter period of the judges (Ruth 1:1). These were dark days, full of suffering brought about by the Israelites' apostasy and immorality. Part of the judgments God brought upon His sinful people included famine and war. The book of Ruth opens with a report of famine, which drove Naomi's family out of Bethlehem into neighboring Moab. Naomi eventually returned with Ruth because she heard "that the Lord had visited His people in giving them food" (1:6).

Readers can identify this interlude as part of the cyclical pattern of sin, suffering, supplication, and salvation found in Judges. But this story stands as a ray of light, showing the power of the love between God and His faithful people. The author gave the reader a snapshot perspective—one family, in a small town, at the threshing floor—as opposed to the broader narratives found in Judges.

Why Is Ruth so Important?

The book was written from Naomi's point of view. Every event related back to her: her husband's and sons' deaths, her daughters-in-law, her return to Bethlehem, her God, her relative, Boaz, her land to sell, and her progeny. Almost without peer in Scripture, this story views "God through the eyes of a woman."[1]

Naomi has been compared to a female Job. She lost everything: home, husband, and sons—and even more than Job did—her livelihood. She joined the ranks of Israel's lowest members: the poor and the widowed. She cried out in her grief and neglected to see the gift that God placed in her path—Ruth.

Ruth herself embodied loyal love. Her moving vow of loyalty (Ruth 1:16–17), though obviously not marital in nature, is often included in modern wedding ceremonies to communicate the depths of devotion to which the new couples aspire. The book reveals the extent of God's grace—He accepted Ruth into His chosen people and honored her with a role in continuing the family line into which His appointed king, David, and later His Son, Jesus, would be born (Matthew 1:1, 5).

What's the Big Idea?

Obedience in everyday life pleases God. When we reflect His character through our interactions with others, we bring glory to Him. Ruth's sacrifice and hard work to provide for Naomi reflected God's love. Boaz's loyalty to his kinsman, Naomi's husband, reflected God's faithfulness. Naomi's plan for Ruth's future reflected selfless love.

The book of Ruth showed the Israelites the blessings that obedience could bring. It showed them the loving, faithful nature of their God. This book demonstrates that God responds to His people's cry. He practices what He preaches, so to speak. Watching Him provide for Naomi and Ruth, two widows with little prospects for a future, we learn that He cares for the outcasts of society just as He asks us to do (Jeremiah 22:16; James 1:27).

How Do I Apply This?

The book of Ruth came along at a time of irresponsible living in Israel's history and appropriately called the people back to a greater responsibility and faithfulness before God—even in difficult times. This call applies just as clearly to us today.

We belong to a loving, faithful, and powerful God who has never failed to care and provide for His children. Like Ruth and Boaz, we are called to respond to that divine grace in faithful obedience, in spite of the godless culture in which we live. Are you willing?

Ruth

JUDGES TURBULENT TIMES	Ruth's Choice	Ruth's Service	Ruth's Claim	Ruth's Marriage	1 SAMUEL CHANGING TIMES
	NAOMI AND RUTH (Mutual grief)	RUTH AND NAOMI AND BOAZ (Mutual pursuit)		BOAZ AND RUTH (Mutual love)	
	"May the LORD grant that you may find rest." (1:9)	Naomi had a kinsman . . . whose name was Boaz. (2:1)	"Wait . . . until you know how the matter turns out." (3:18)	Boaz took Ruth, and she became his wife. (4:13)	"Blessed is the LORD who has not left you without a redeemer today." (4:14)
	CHAPTER 1	*CHAPTER 2*	*CHAPTER 3*	*CHAPTER 4*	
Setting	"Now it came about in the days when the judges governed, that there was a famine in the land" (1:1).				
Circumstance	Loss — deeper commitment		Gain — deeper love		
Emotion	Grief	Loneliness	Companionship	Rejoicing	
Theme	Redemption: God provides for those who trust Him in hard times.				
Key Verses	1:16; 3:11–12				
Christ in Ruth	Prefigured in the kinsman-redeemer				

FIRST SAMUEL

Who Wrote the Book?

Together, 1 and 2 Samuel form one book in the Hebrew Bible. The Greek translation of the Bible, the Septuagint, was the first version to divide the material into two parts. (See Appendix D for more information on the Septuagint.) Though named after its main character, the prophet Samuel, the book does not claim an author. However, Samuel may have written, and he certainly supplied, the information for 1 Samuel 1:1–24:22, which is a biography of his life and career up to his death. First Chronicles 29:29 notes that Samuel, along with Nathan and Gad, recorded the "acts of King David." Evidence in the writing suggests that the books of 1 and 2 Samuel were compiled by someone from the prophetic school who used documents from Samuel, Nathan, and Gad.[1]

Where Are We?

First Samuel 27:6 refers to the divided monarchy, when the ten tribes of Israel rebelled against the two tribes of Judah, which occurred after Solomon's reign. From this we can conclude that the book came together sometime after the death of David (971 BC) and perhaps even after the death of Solomon (931 BC). Because the book contains no reference to the Assyrian invasion in 722 BC, it likely originated before the period of the exile.

The events that happen in 1 Samuel took place over a period of about 110 years, stretching from the closing days of the judges, when Samuel was born (ca. 1120 BC) through the death of Saul (1011 BC). We see the birth of Samuel, his call from God and subsequent prophetic ministry, the rise and fall of King Saul, and the anointing and maturity of young David.

First Samuel is set in the land of Israel, where the Hebrews invaded and settled (see Joshua). Numerous other peoples continued to dwell alongside Israel, often disrupting the peace and encouraging the Israelites to stray from their faith.

Why Is First Samuel so Important?

In this critical period of Israel's history, the people of God transformed from a loosely affiliated group of tribes into a unified nation under a form of government headed by a king. They traded the turmoil of life under the judges for the stability of a strong central monarchy. (See Map of the United Kingdom in Appendix A for a visual representation of Israel under the monarchy.)

First Samuel focuses on the establishment of that monarchy. The people demanded a king, similar to the kings of the surrounding nations (1 Samuel 8:5). Saul, the first king, though "head and shoulders above the rest" did not have a righteous heart, and his line was destined never to inherit the crown (9:1–15:35). God instructed Samuel to anoint David, the youngest son of Jesse of Bethlehem, as the next king (16:1–13).

Much of 1 Samuel follows David's exploits as a young musician, shepherd, and warrior. We witness his underdog victory over Goliath (17:1–58), his deep friendship with Jonathan (18:1–4), and his growing military prowess (18:5–30). He waited patiently for the throne, often pursued and driven into hiding by Saul. The book concludes with Saul's death (31:1–13), which serves as a natural dividing marker between 1 Samuel and 2 Samuel.

What's the Big Idea?

First Samuel chronicles the beginning of Israel's monarchy, following the lives of the prophet Samuel, the ill-fated King Saul, and God's ultimate choice of David as king. Several themes feature prominently.

Providence: God repeatedly made everyday events work for His purposes. He used Hannah's contentious relationship with Peninnah (1 Samuel 1:1–28), led Saul to Samuel during Saul's search for lost donkeys (9:1–27), and caused David to learn of Goliath while taking food to his brothers (17:1–58). These are but a few examples.

Kingship: As the divine King, God designated a human vice-regent, David, to rule over His people. This history validates David's house as the legitimate rulers of Israel. It also fulfills Jacob's promise that the scepter will never depart from Judah, David's tribe (Genesis 49:10).

Reversal of human fortune: Hannah's barrenness gave way to children (1 Samuel 1:1–28; 2:21); Samuel became prophet instead of Eli's sons (2:12; 3:13); Saul rose to prominence though he was from a lowly tribe; and David was anointed king though he was the youngest son (16:1–13). Normal human patterns were reversed by God so that His plan could be furthered, showing His sovereignty over all.

How Do I Apply This?

God is still sovereign in the twenty-first century. He will accomplish His purposes with or without our cooperation. But as was true in the lives of Samuel, Saul, and David, our response to God's call affects our outcome. Will we obey Him as Samuel and David did and live lives marked by blessing? Or will we, like Saul, try to live on our own terms? "To obey is better than sacrifice," Samuel told Saul (1 Samuel 15:22). That truth still speaks to us today.

First Samuel

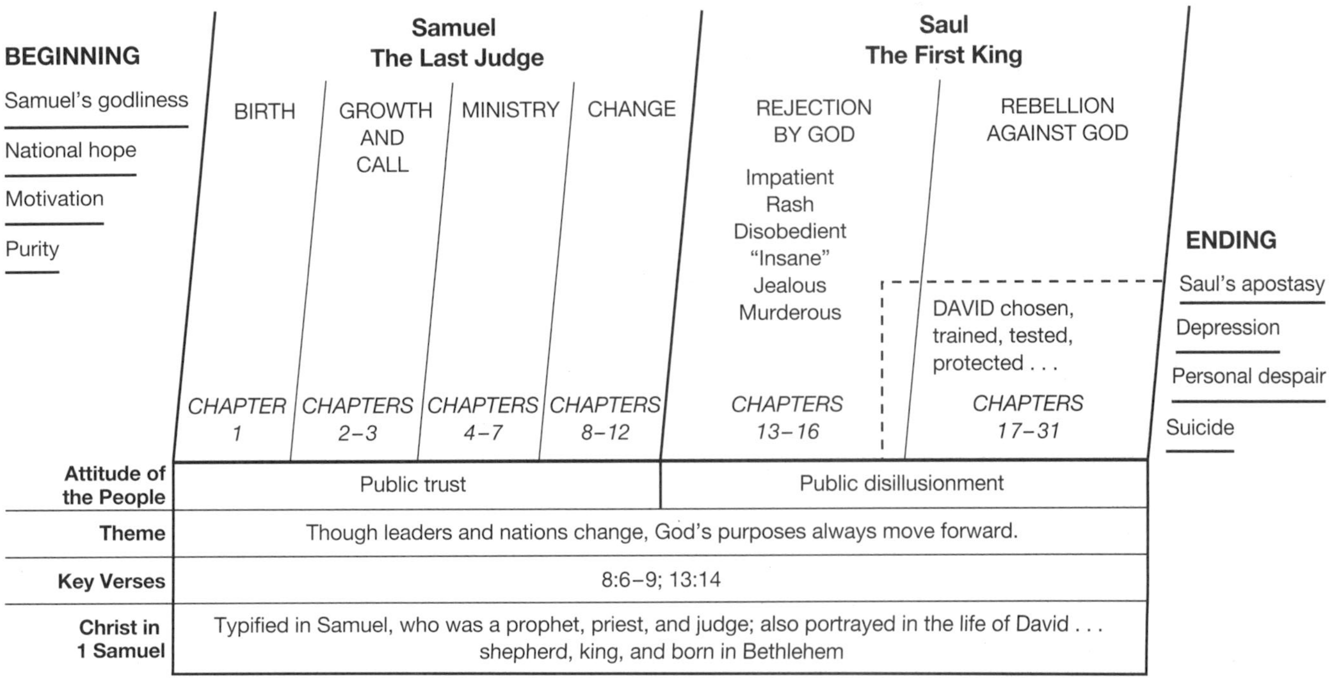

	Samuel The Last Judge				Saul The First King	
BEGINNING Samuel's godliness National hope Motivation Purity	BIRTH	GROWTH AND CALL	MINISTRY	CHANGE	REJECTION BY GOD Impatient Rash Disobedient "Insane" Jealous Murderous	REBELLION AGAINST GOD DAVID chosen, trained, tested, protected . . .
	CHAPTER 1	*CHAPTERS 2–3*	*CHAPTERS 4–7*	*CHAPTERS 8–12*	*CHAPTERS 13–16*	*CHAPTERS 17–31*
Attitude of the People	Public trust				Public disillusionment	
Theme	Though leaders and nations change, God's purposes always move forward.					
Key Verses	8:6–9; 13:14					
Christ in 1 Samuel	Typified in Samuel, who was a prophet, priest, and judge; also portrayed in the life of David . . . shepherd, king, and born in Bethlehem					

ENDING

Saul's apostasy

Depression

Personal despair

Suicide

SECOND SAMUEL

Who Wrote the Book?

As we noted in the previous chapter, 1 and 2 Samuel form one book in the Hebrew Bible. The Septuagint, the Greek version of the Bible, first divided these books into two parts. Although the book does not name a specific author, the material was compiled from documents written and collected by the prophets Nathan, Gad, and Samuel—the prophet for whom the book is named (1 Chronicles 29:29).

Where Are We?

Second Samuel is set in the land of Israel during the reign of David and follows the course of his forty years as king of Israel (1011–971 BC).

Why Is Second Samuel so Important?

First Samuel introduces the monarchy of Israel, and 2 Samuel chronicles the establishment of the Davidic dynasty and the expansion of Israel under God's chosen leader. The book opens as David learned of Saul's death. His lament over the deaths of Saul and of Jonathan (2 Samuel 1:19–27), David's unlikely best friend, demonstrated David's personal grief over their demise. The Lord soon set David over the tribe of Judah (2:4) and then over all Israel as His anointed king (5:3), uniting all twelve tribes into a tight-knit nation.

The first ten chapters show David as victorious in battle, praised by the people, compassionate to the sick and poor, and righteous in God's sight. We see David dance before the Lord in the streets of Jerusalem as his men brought the ark of the covenant back home (6:12–16). We also meet Mephibosheth, the crippled son of Jonathan to whom David extended grace, "for the sake of [his] father Jonathan" (9:7).

Yet biblical writers did not overlook their heroes' flaws. In the chapters that follow, we note that David's adultery with Bathsheba (2 Samuel 11:1–27) was followed by a series of tragedies: their child's death (12:18), David's daughter Tamar's rape by his son Amnon (13:1–39), Amnon's murder (13:28–30), David's own political overthrow by his son Absalom (15:1–37), and Absalom's subsequent death (18:1–33).

Despite the turmoil in his later years, David enjoyed the Lord's forgiveness and favor. His genuine sorrow and regret over his sins revealed his repentant heart, with which the Lord was pleased.

What's the Big Idea?

Key to the book and to the entire biblical record is 2 Samuel 7:16, "Your house and your kingdom shall endure before Me forever; your throne shall be established forever." This divine promise marked the beginning of an additional covenant, called the Davidic covenant, in which God promised an eternal throne to the house of David. "Because of David's faith, God did not treat [David's] descendants as He had treated Saul's. Sin would be punished, but David's line would never be completely cut off."[1]

David celebrated God's faithfulness in Psalm 89, penning these words inspired by God:

> "My covenant I will not violate,
> Nor will I alter the utterance of My lips.
> Once I have sworn by My holiness;
> I will not lie to David.
> His descendants shall endure forever
> And his throne as the sun before Me.
> It shall be established forever like the moon,
> And the witness in the sky is faithful." (Psalm 89:34–37)

God's unconditional promise to David would be fulfilled ultimately in David's descendant Jesus Christ. The covenant also included a continuing promise that the people of Israel would have a land of their own forever.

How Do I Apply This?

David is known as a "man after [God's] own heart" (1 Samuel 13:14) because, though he sinned greatly and made mistakes, he acknowledged those failures and repented before God. *Repent* means to turn away from sin and turn toward righteousness. Our Father knows we are not perfect. So His Son, Jesus Christ, paid the price for our sins so that we can become righteous in God's sight through faith. And although our salvation is secure, our daily sins can hinder our relationship with God. When we confess our sins, turning to the Lord in humility, He will forgive us and restore our relationship with Him.

The apostle James has written what might be an appropriate epitaph for David. It can be yours, too: "Humble yourselves in the presence of the Lord, and He will exalt you" (James 4:10).

Second Samuel

	David's Triumphs		David's Troubles			Appendix
	Reigning in Hebron over Judea	Reigning in Jerusalem over all Israel	With himself	With his family	With his nation	Miscellaneous narratives
	David's lament (1) David's crowning (2) David's increase (3–4)	A new capital (5) A new worship center (6) A new dynasty (7) A new boundary (8) A new son (9) Another new boundary (10)	David's sin (11) Nathan's denunciation (12)	Amnon's immorality (13) Absalom's crime and flight (14) Absalom's revolt (15) Absalom's counselors (16–17) Absalom's death (18)	David's return (19) Sheba's revolt (20)	A famine (21) A song (22) A prophecy (23) A failure (24)
	CHAPTERS 1–4	*CHAPTERS 5–10*	*CHAPTERS 11–12*	*CHAPTERS 13–18*	*CHAPTERS 19–20*	*CHAPTERS 21–24*
Theme	Blessings or consequences follow every action.					
Key Verses	7:12–13					
Christ in 2 Samuel	Foreshadowed in David's reign, which, though imperfect, is characterized by justice, wisdom, and integrity; the Messiah, the Son of David, is promised as an offspring of the Davidic line and One who will sit upon David's throne forever.					

FIRST KINGS

Who Wrote the Book?

Like the books of 1 and 2 Samuel, 1 and 2 Kings originally were one book. In the Hebrew Bible the book of Kings continued the narrative started in Samuel. The Septuagint separated them into two parts. We derive our English title "Kings" from Jerome's Vulgate, the Latin translation of the Bible. (See Appendix D for more information about the Vulgate.)

No one knows the author of 1 and 2 Kings, though some commentators have suggested Ezra, Ezekiel, and Jeremiah as possible authors. Because the entire work encompasses a time period of more than four hundred years, several source materials were used to compile the records. Certain clues such as literary styles, themes woven throughout the book, and the nature of material used point to a single compiler or author rather than multiple compilers or authors. This person assembled the manuscript while God's people were in exile at Babylon (see next chapter). But he didn't complete the work until the Babylonians released King Jehoiachin after thirty-seven years in prison (560 BC), most likely completing it within another twenty years.[1]

Where Are We?

First Kings opens describing the final days of King David (around 971 BC) and the conspiracies surrounding his succession. When David died (1 Kings 2:10), Solomon ascended the throne and established himself as a strong and wise leader. In the early years of Solomon's reign, Israel experienced its "glory days." Its influence, economy, and military power enjoyed little opposition; its neighbors posed no strong military threat.

Shortly after Solomon's death in 931 BC (1 Kings 11:43), the kingdom was divided into northern (Israel) and southern (Judah) entities. The Map of the Divided Kingdom in Appendix A shows the geographic boundaries of each kingdom. First Kings follows the history of this divided kingdom through the year 853 BC.

Why Is First Kings so Important?

Those kings who reigned under God's authority—who remained faithful to the Law—experienced God's blessings. But those kings who deviated from the Law experienced curses.

First Kings reveals Solomon's relationship with Yahweh, emphasizing Solomon's divinely given wisdom and wealth. Solomon's reputation reached far beyond Israel's borders to modern-day Yemen, the queen of Sheba's likely home (1 Kings 10:1–13). Solomon's numerous marriages and extensive harem are the stuff of legends, but they led to his wandering faith in later years. Solomon did, however, build the temple, God's permanent dwelling place among His people.

First Kings also introduces the prophet Elijah, who pronounced God's judgment on the evil northern king Ahab. In addition to performing other miracles, Elijah won a dramatic confrontation with false prophets on Mount Carmel (18:1–46).

What's the Big Idea?

First Kings was written "to record history but, more important, to teach the *lessons* of history."[2] As with other historical books in the Old Testament, the history recorded here was meant to preserve not just important events but spiritual truths learned through those events.

In the books of 1 and 2 Kings, each king is evaluated by "his reaction toward his covenantal responsibility to the Law of the Lord. That was the acid test of whether he 'did evil' or 'that which was right in the eyes of the Lord.'"[3] Readers will notice scathing rebukes of some kings—reports not typically recorded by purely historical writers. In addition to the kings, the prophets figure heavily in this book. They are God's spokesmen, proclaiming His word to mostly hard-hearted rulers. It is through the prophets' eyes—always connecting the nation's fortune with its kings' faithfulness (or lack thereof)—that we learn the history of Israel and Judah.

How Do I Apply This?

Solomon was known as the wisest man of his day. He was arguably the wealthiest man of his time. He enjoyed God's favor in many ways, yet his legacy is tarnished by the faithlessness he displayed in his later years. In direct contradiction to God's command for a king not to "multiply wives" (Deuteronomy 17:17), Solomon married many foreign women. First Kings laments, "When Solomon was old, his wives turned his heart away after other gods" (11:4). Solomon began to rely on his fortune, his military might, and his political alliances instead of the God who gave all of those blessings to him. He focused on the gifts, forgetting the Giver.

How often do you do the same? Are there any direct commands from God you are ignoring? Today, take time to recall the blessings in your life, and then thank the Lord for them. Rely on Him, not your possessions or position, as your source of strength and significance.

> Some trust in chariots and some in horses, but we trust in the name of the LORD our God. (Psalm 20:7 NIV)

First Kings

	Solomon **"In all his glory" (Luke 12:27)**	Decline and Demise	Disruption **"A kingdom divided against itself" (Mark 3:24)**	
POLITICALLY David succeeded by Solomon NATIONALLY Kingdom united ECONOMICALLY Solid and secure SPIRITUALLY Shaky	Crowned and inaugurated (1–2) Married and exalted (3–4) Temple erected and dedicated (5–8) Warned and blessed (9–10)		Internal conflict and hostility (12–14) Civil war and idolatry (15–16) Ahab and Elijah (17–22) "He served Baal and worshiped him and provoked the LORD God of Israel to anger, according to all that his father had done" (22:53).	POLITICALLY King after king NATIONALLY Kingdom divided ECONOMICALLY Unstable SPIRITUALLY Empty
	CHAPTERS 1–10	*CHAPTER 11*	*CHAPTERS 12–22*	

Time	40 years	80 years
Kingdom	United and strong	Divided and weak
People	Solomon	Jeroboam to Ahaziah Rehoboam to Jehoshaphat
Identity	"All Israel . . . sons of Israel"	North: Israel; Samaria; Ephraim South: Judah; Jerusalem
Theme	Spiritual and moral decay lead to destruction.	
Key Verses	9:3–9; 11:11–13	
Christ in 1 Kings	Solomon's wisdom, which foreshadows Him who "became to us wisdom from God" (1 Corinthians 1:30); the prophetic ministry and miracles of Elijah	

SECOND KINGS

Who Wrote the Book?

As we noted in the previous chapter, 1 and 2 Kings originally comprised one book of history. The author is neither indicated in the text nor known by scholars. He was most likely a prophet, because many of the historical events were recorded in light of Israel's and Judah's faithfulness—or unfaithfulness—to their covenant with God. Ezra, Ezekiel, and Jeremiah have all been named as possible authors.

Where Are We?

Second Kings continues the history of the divided kingdom, picking up the story around 853 BC. In 722 BC, the powerful nation of Assyria invaded the northern kingdom, scattering and taking captive the people of Israel. Only Judah remained intact. But then Assyria suffered a stunning fall to the Babylonians, who took the Assyrian capital of Nineveh in 612 BC. By 605 BC Babylon dominated Judah, had taken some captives away, and in 586 BC Babylon destroyed Jerusalem and took additional prisoners into captivity. Many people who were considered valuable to the invaders, such as the prophet Daniel and members of the royal family, were taken to Babylon early on. By the end of Kings, the people of God no longer inhabited their Promised Land. Many areas of the country had been rendered virtually uninhabitable due to the razing, burning, and other destructive tactics of the Babylonian army, while the people had been enslaved, scattered, and decimated by their enemies.

The book ends with an epilogue of sorts, giving a peek into the good fortune of Jehoiachin—Judah's last true ruler before a series of puppet kings were installed by Babylon. If Jeremiah did write much of Kings, he could not have written this section, set in Babylon, for he had been taken away to Egypt years earlier.

Why Is Second Kings so Important?

Second Kings features many unique events and people. Two people were raised from the dead (2 Kings 4:32–37; 13:20–21). The prophet Elijah left this earth without dying (2:1–18); Enoch was the only other man in the Bible to do so (Genesis 5:21–24). The waters of the Jordan River rolled back twice (2 Kings 2:8, 14). These and other miraculous events testify to God's continuing work among His people.

The time period covered by this book saw the emergence of the first writing prophets in Israel. Amos and Hosea went to the people of Israel, while Isaiah, Joel, Micah, Nahum, Habbakuk, Zephaniah, and Jeremiah prophesied in Judah, both groups calling the people to repentance and warning them of God's coming judgments. The author devoted extensive space to Elisha's ministry after Elijah was taken to heaven, giving special attention to the numerous miracles Elisha performed.

None of the kings of Israel are described as having done right in God's eyes; each led the people deeper into idolatry. Several of Judah's kings were righteous, notably Joash, Uzziah, Hezekiah, and Josiah. Hezekiah held off the Assyrians by trusting in the Lord for deliverance. Josiah later instituted an even greater spiritual reformation. Neither effort, however, was enough to stem God's eventual judgment on the nation in fulfillment of the curses of the Mosaic Covenant (Deuteronomy 28).

What's the Big Idea?

World affairs played a heavy role in Israel's and Judah's destinies. Yet, the author of 2 Kings directly connected the Israelites' apostasy—led by their wicked kings—to their national destruction, pointing it out as God's judgment on His wayward children. Despite repeated warnings from God's prophets to turn from their ways and return to God, the people continued to live in sin. To their regret, they did not believe that God would allow their nation to be ruined by foreign invaders.

Yet God did not forget His promise to David, either. God saved a remnant from among the people and kept the royal line intact so that one day His people could return to their land to await the promised Redeemer.

How Do I Apply This?

Second Kings teaches an important life lesson: actions have consequences. "Repent! Sin will incur judgment," God warned in effect through the prophets. Israel and Judah learned the hard way that God means what He says.

How will *we* learn? Consider your heart. Is it hard, resistant to God's call? Or can you acknowledge your sin and turn back to Him?

SECOND KINGS

	Northern Kingdom Israel	Both Kingdoms (Alternating)	Southern Kingdom Judah
	ISRAEL'S FALL TO ASSYRIA 722 BC	JUDAH'S FALL TO BABYLON 586 BC	
	CHAPTERS 1–10	CHAPTERS 11–17	CHAPTERS 18–25
Northern Prophets	Elijah Elisha	Jonah Amos Hosea	
Southern Prophets		Obadiah Joel Micah Isaiah	Nahum Zephaniah Jeremiah Habakkuk
Northern Kings	Ahaziah to Hoshea		
Southern Kings		Jehoram to Zedekiah	
Key Chapters	17 and 25		
Theme	God is patient, but He does not allow persistent sin to go unpunished.		
Key Verses	17:22–23		
Christ in 2 Kings	Foreshadowed in the faithfulnes of some Judean kings; seen in the healing ministry and compassion of Elisha		

FIRST CHRONICLES

Who Wrote the Book?

"The chronicler," as scholars have long referred to the author of this book, is anonymous. Jewish tradition speculates that Ezra could have written 1 and 2 Chronicles, which—like Samuel and Kings—originally formed one work. But nothing within the text provides a definitive clue as to the compiler of the material.

Several indications throughout the book reveal the author's reliance on a variety of source materials—"annals," "books," and "records"—which are cited as dependable historical documentation. "Whoever the author was, he was a meticulous historian who carefully utilized official and unofficial documents."[1]

Where Are We?

The time frame covered in 1 Chronicles mirrors parts of 2 Samuel and 1 Kings. The chronicler focused on David's reign in 1 Chronicles, including and omitting different events recorded in the other biblical histories, so that his document recorded those events significant to his purpose. For instance, 1 Chronicles does not include David's adultery with Bathsheba (2 Samuel 11), which was a well-known fact even before the chronicler began his work, and so it did not bear repeating.

Chronicles was most likely written during the time of Ezra or Nehemiah, while the Jews were dispersed throughout Persia, some having returned to Israel. Archaeological evidence supports this premise. "Fragments of an actual manuscript of Chronicles found at Qumran makes a date in the Persian period (538–333 BC) almost certain."[2]

Why Is First Chronicles so Important?

Readers will note the extensive space devoted to genealogies. Why are these family lists so common in Chronicles? Scholars say that genealogies serve many purposes, among them

> To demonstrate the legitimacy of a person or family's claim to a particular role or rank . . . to preserve the purity of the chosen people and/or its priesthood . . . to affirm the continuity of the people of God despite expulsion from the Promised Land.[3]

In addition to family history, 1 Chronicles lists priests, Levites, armies, temple officials, and other leaders of various ministries.

In Chronicles, the history of Israel is told through a priestly perspective. The chronicler devoted significant attention to proper worship of Yahweh and adherence to the regulations of His Law. The author included David's decisions on the proper manner in which to undertake moving the ark of the covenant (1 Chronicles 13, 15–16) and detailed descriptions of its return to Jerusalem. The chronicler even highlighted one of David's psalms (16:8–36). We read the story of how David purchased the threshing floor of Ornan the Jebusite, which he then designated as the future site of the temple (21:15–30). Though David desired to build the temple, God revealed to him that David's son Solomon would have that honor (17:1–14).

What's the Big Idea?

Why do we need the books of 1–2 Chronicles when we already have the history of 2 Samuel and 1–2 Kings? Just as the gospels of Matthew, Mark, Luke, and John each offer a different perspective on the life of Jesus, so the books of Chronicles present Israel's history with a purpose different than the other historical books. The books of 2 Samuel and 1–2 Kings reveal the monarchies of Israel and Judah—in particular the sins of the nations that resulted in the exile. But the books of Chronicles, written *after* the time of the exile, focus on those elements of history that

God wanted the returning Jews to meditate upon: obedience that results in God's blessing, the priority of the temple and priesthood, and the unconditional promises to the house of David.

David's prayer in 1 Chronicles 29:10–19 summarizes the themes the chronicler wished to communicate: glory to God, gratitude for gifting David's family with leadership of the nation, and the desire that David's descendants continue to devote themselves to God. Remaining faithful to God would reap blessing.

When the book was written, David's descendants no longer ruled as monarchs over Israel. But the chronicler desired the people to remember the royal Davidic lineage, for God had promised a future ruler would rise from that line. After the seventy-year exile in Babylon, Jewish political and social power resided more with the religious rather than political rulers. Telling Israel's history through a priestly and kingly lens was intended to prepare the people for a future Messiah.

How Do I Apply This?

Read David's magnificent prayer in 1 Chronicles 29. Consider your own spiritual heritage. Would you like to model such godly strength and character as his to your own children? What steps do you need to take in order to echo truthfully David's attitude in verse 11, "Yours, O Lord, is the greatness and the power and the glory and the majesty and the splendor, for everything in heaven and earth is yours" (NIV)?

Knowing that He tests the heart and is pleased with integrity (1 Chronicles 29:17), ask the Spirit to fill you daily and guide your steps that future generations might be blessed.

First and Second Chronicles

	1 Chronicles God's View: Chosen			2 Chronicles . . . and Preserved	
	GENEALOGIES	SAUL	DAVID AND THE TEMPLE	SOLOMON The King Glory	JUDAH The Nation REVIVAL REJECTION
	CHAPTERS 1–9	*CHAPTER 10*	*CHAPTERS 11–29*	*CHAPTERS 1–9*	*CHAPTERS 10–36*
Process	Little made great			Great becoming little	
Emphasis	Personal determination			National deterioration	
History	Creation of world to creation of kingdom			Solomon's temple to rebuilding of the temple	
Theme	The temple — the structural state of the temple corresponds to the spiritual state of the people.				
Key Verses	1 Chronicles 17; 29:10–13; 2 Chronicles 7:12–22; 16:9				
Christ in Chronicles	Christ is foretold in the Davidic Covenant (1 Chronicles 17) and prefigured in the idealized kings David and Solomon; also the ark and the temple typify Christ's power and presence with us.				

CONSECRATION — RESTORATION

SECOND CHRONICLES

Who Wrote the Book?

A post-exilic (after the exile) Jewish scholar compiled material from many historical resources to chronicle the history of his people. This person is not named and remains unknown, though Ezra has been cited as a possible candidate. Whoever "the chronicler" was, he utilized official and unofficial documents to write this historical account. As noted earlier, 2 Chronicles originally was joined with 1 Chronicles as one book, separated into two books since about 200 BC when the Septuagint, the Greek version of the Old Testament, was translated.

Where Are We?

Second Chronicles covers the time from Solomon's ascension to the throne (971 BC) until the southern kingdom of Judah was finally carried into exile in Babylon in 586 BC. The focus of the book is on Judah. The author was more concerned with telling the story of David's descendants, who reigned over Judah, than with the history of the northern kingdom of Israel. The centrality of Jerusalem, where the temple was located, falls in line with the book's overarching focus on the priesthood as well.

Again, 2 Chronicles was probably written in the fifth century BC, "following the return of a small group of Jews to Judah following the fall of the Babylonian Empire. Intent on rebuilding the temple and resettling the Holy Land, the little community soon found itself in a struggle simply to survive."[1] The Jews eventually rebuilt the temple but languished for years in their fight to reclaim the land. Against this backdrop, the chronicler portrayed Jewish history, focusing on the blessings God bestowed when leaders were faithful to His Law.

Why Is Second Chronicles so Important?

The book opens with Solomon establishing his throne over a unified nation, solidifying his authority and squashing early rebellions (1 Kings 2). He then built the magnificent temple of God, using the plans God gave to his father, David. Six of the nine chapters devoted to King Solomon focus on the temple construction, a task reserved for him since before his birth (2 Chronicles 2–7).

When the kingdom split under the rule of Rehoboam, Solomon's son, the Levites from all over Israel sided with Rehoboam and flocked to Jerusalem to continue their priestly duties (10:1–19). But a cycle of righteousness and corruption characterized the throne. Some kings were completely evil, disregarding God's Law and leading the people into sinful behaviors. A few kings, such as Solomon, started off as righteous but fell away. Others strayed but repented, such as Manassah (33:1–25). A few kings, such as Hezekiah and Josiah, were honored with the epitaph "he did right in the sight of the Lord" (29:2; 34:2). Throughout 2 Chronicles, faithfulness was rewarded; betrayal was judged.

A history lover will enjoy the numerous mentions of secular historical figures during this time period. From Tilgath-pilneser of Assyria, to Sennacherib of Assyria, to Nebuchadnezzar of Babylon, non-Jewish foreign leaders played prominent roles in the political fortunes of Judah.

What's the Big Idea?

The post-exilic Jews needed a reminder of who their God was and how He worked. History provided the best lesson for them. "The author uses the history of Judah to demonstrate that God blesses His people when they remain faithful and joyfully worship the Lord."[2]

One writer stated that:

> History itself is a call to worship and an invitation to hope. If the struggling community of Jews in Judah will put God first as did godly generations of the past, and show their commitment by a similar zeal for worship,

> the Lord will surely show His faithfulness to them. The line of David will yet again take Zion's throne and the kingdom of God be established over all the earth.[3]

How Do I Apply This?

As it did for the Israelites, history can jog our memories. Can you remember times when God blessed you? Such memories are blessings in themselves, as well as encouragements to press on in holiness, with hope and confidence.

If you are hard-pressed to recall specific times when God worked in your life, consider your devotional habits. A prayer journal that recalls prayers asked and those answered can act as your own "history" manual. God wants us to remember His works, so we, too, can praise Him for His goodness and have hope for our future!

First and Second Chronicles

	1 Chronicles God's View: Chosen			2 Chronicles . . . and Preserved	
	GENEALOGIES	SAUL	DAVID AND THE TEMPLE	SOLOMON The King	JUDAH The Nation
				Glory	REVIVAL / REJECTION
	CHAPTERS 1–9	*CHAPTER 10*	*CHAPTERS 11–29*	*CHAPTERS 1–9*	*CHAPTERS 10–36*
Process	Little made great			Great becoming little	
Emphasis	Personal determination			National deterioration	
History	Creation of world to creation of kingdom			Solomon's temple to rebuilding of the temple	
Theme	The temple — the structural state of the temple corresponds to the spiritual state of the people.				
Key Verses	1 Chronicles 17; 29:10–13; 2 Chronicles 7:12–22; 16:9				
Christ in Chronicles	Christ is foretold in the Davidic Covenant (1 Chronicles 17) and prefigured in the idealized kings David and Solomon; also the ark and the temple typify Christ's power and presence with us.				

CONSECRATION — RESTORATION

EZRA

Who Wrote the Book?

Jewish tradition has long attributed authorship of this historical book to the scribe and scholar Ezra, who led the second group of Jews returning from Babylon to Jerusalem (Ezra 7:11–26). Ezra 8 includes a first-person reference, implying the author's participation in the events. He plays a major role in the second half of the book, as well as in the book of Nehemiah, its sequel. In the Hebrew Bible, the two books were considered one work, though some internal evidence suggests they were written separately and joined together in the Hebrew canon (and separated again in English translations).

Ezra was a direct descendant of Aaron the chief priest (7:1–5), thus he was a priest and scribe in his own right. His zeal for God and God's Law spurred Ezra to lead a group of Jews back to Israel during King Artaxerxes's reign over the Persian Empire (which had since replaced the Babylonian Empire that originally exiled the people of Judah).

Where Are We?

The book of Ezra records two separate time periods directly following the seventy years of Babylonian captivity. Ezra 1–6 covers the first return of Jews from captivity, led by Zerubbabel—a period of twenty-three years beginning with the edict of Cyrus of Persia and ending at the rebuilding of the temple in Jerusalem (538–515 BC). Ezra 7–10 picks up the story more than sixty years later, when Ezra led the second group of exiles to Israel (458 BC). The book could not have been completed earlier than about 450 BC (the date of the events recorded in 10:17–44). (See Map of the Exile and Returns in Appendix A to see the journey the exiles made back to Jerusalem.)

The events in Ezra are set in Jerusalem and the surrounding area. The returning exiles were able to populate only a tiny portion of their former homeland.

Why Is Ezra so Important?

The book of Ezra provides a much-needed link in the historical record of the Israelite people. When their king was dethroned and captured and the people exiled to Babylon, Judah as an independent nation ceased to exist. The book of Ezra provides an account of the Jews' regathering, of their struggle to survive and to rebuild what had been destroyed. Through his narrative, Ezra declared that they were still God's people and that God had not forgotten them.

In the book of Ezra we witness the rebuilding of the new temple, the unification of the returning tribes as they shared common struggles and were challenged to work together. Later, after the original remnant had stopped work on the city walls and spiritual apathy ruled, Ezra arrived with another two thousand people and sparked a spiritual revival. By the end of the book, Israel had renewed its covenant with God and had begun acting in obedience to Him.

Ezra also contains one of the great intercessory prayers of the Bible (Ezra 9:5–15; see Daniel 9 and Nehemiah 9 for others). His leadership proved crucial to the Jews' spiritual advancement.

What's the Big Idea?

Ezra's narrative reveals two main issues faced by the returning exiles: (1) the struggle to restore the temple (Ezra 1:1–6:22) and (2) the need for spiritual reformation (7:1–10:44). Both were necessary in order for the people to renew their fellowship with the Lord.

A broader theological purpose is also revealed: God keeps His promises. Through the prophets, God had ordained that His chosen people would return to their land after a seventy-year exile. Ezra's account proclaims that God kept His word, and it shows that when God's people remained faithful to Him, He would continue to bless them. Hence, the book emphasizes the temple and proper worship, similar to Chronicles (which was also written during these days).

How Do I Apply This?

God moved the hearts of secular rulers (Cyrus, Darius, and Artaxerxes) to allow, even encourage and help, the Jewish people to return home. He used these unlikely allies to fulfill His promises of restoration for His chosen people. Have you encountered unlikely sources of blessing? Have you wondered how God can really work all things together for the good of those who are called by His name (Romans 8:28)? Take time today to acknowledge God's sovereignty and mercy in your life. Recommit to Him your trust, your love, and your obedience.

EZRA

	CHRONICLES	Construction Leader: Zerubbabel		ESTHER	Reformation Leader: Ezra		NEHEMIAH
		CENSUS AND JOURNEY	Temple Foundation Opposition Determination Completion		CENSUS AND JOURNEY	Revival Condition Confession Covenant Cleansing	
		CHAPTERS 1–2	*CHAPTERS 3–6*		*CHAPTERS 7–8*	*CHAPTERS 9–10*	
Emphasis		Construction of the temple		XERXES	Reformation of the people		
Persian King		Cyrus	Darius		Artaxerxes		
Scope		National	General		Personal	Specific	
Theme		Revival and reformation					
Key Verses		1:1–4; 3:2; 7:10					
Christ in Ezra		His birth anticipated in the preservation of the Davidic line and the remnant's return to the Promised Land; His work as spiritual rebuilder and restorer pictured in Zerubbabel and Ezra; His mediating presence and glory pictured in the altar and the temple					

NEHEMIAH

Who Wrote the Book?

Jewish tradition identifies Nehemiah himself as the primary author of this historical book. Much of the book is written from his first-person perspective. Nothing is known about his youth or background; we meet him as an adult serving in the Persian royal court as the personal cupbearer to King Artaxerxes (Nehemiah 1:11–2:1). This prestigious position reveals something of Nehemiah's upright character. Though he remained in Persia after the exiles had been allowed to go home, he was highly interested in the state of affairs in Judah (his brother Hanani [1:2] had returned there earlier).

The book of Nehemiah could be read as a sequel to the book of Ezra, and some scholars believe the two were originally one work. It is possible that Ezra compiled Nehemiah's original accounts with other material to create the book of Nehemiah. However, most scholars believe the book was written by Nehemiah.

Where Are We?

The book of Nehemiah opens in the Persian city of Susa in the year 444 BC. Later that year, Nehemiah traveled to Israel, leading the third of three returns by the Jewish people following their seventy years of exile in Babylon. (The previous chapter on Ezra describes the earlier two returns.) Most of the book centers on events in Jerusalem. The narrative concludes around the year 430 BC, and scholars believe the book was written shortly thereafter.

Nehemiah is the last historical book of the Old Testament. Although the book of Esther appears after Nehemiah in the canon, the events in

Esther occurred in the time period between Ezra 6 and 7, between the first and second returns of the people to Israel. The prophet Malachi was a contemporary of Nehemiah.

Why Is Nehemiah so Important?

Nehemiah was a layman, not a priest like Ezra nor a prophet like Malachi. He served the Persian king in a secular position before leading a group of Jews to Jerusalem in order to rebuild the city walls. "Nehemiah's expertise in the king's court equipped him adequately for the political and physical reconstruction necessary for the remnant to survive."[1]

Under Nehemiah's leadership, the Jews withstood opposition and came together to accomplish their goal. Nehemiah led by example, giving up a respected position in a palace for hard labor in a politically insignificant district. He partnered with Ezra, who also appears in this book, to solidify the political and spiritual foundations of the people. Nehemiah's humility before God (see his moving intercessory prayers in chapters 1 and 9) provided an example for the people. He did not claim glory for himself but always gave God the credit for his successes.

What's the Big Idea?

Nehemiah recorded the reconstruction of the wall of Jerusalem, Judah's capital city. Together, he and Ezra, who led the spiritual revival of the people, directed the political and religious restoration of the Jews in their homeland after the Babylonian captivity.

Nehemiah's life provides a fine study on leadership. He overcame opposition from outsiders as well as internal turmoil. He exercised his administrative skills in his strategy to use half the people for building while the other half kept watch for the Samaritans who, under Sanballat, threatened attack (Nehemiah 4–7). As governor, Nehemiah negotiated peace among the Jews who were unhappy with Persian taxes. He exhibited a steadfast determination to complete his goals. Accomplishing those goals resulted in a people encouraged, renewed, and excited about their future.

How Do I Apply This?

The book of Nehemiah shows us the kind of significant impact one individual can have on a nation. Nehemiah served in secular offices, using his position to bring back to the Jews order, stability, and proper focus on God.

God uses all manner of people in all manner of places doing all manner of work. Do you feel you must be "in ministry" in order to serve God? Be encouraged; He is not limited by your vocation. In fact, God has placed you where you are for a purpose. Have this attitude about your work: "Whatever you do in word or deed, do all in the name of the Lord Jesus, giving thanks through Him to God the Father" (Colossians 3:17).

NEHEMIAH

	Cupbearer to the King	Builder of the Wall	Governor of the People	
	Prayer May I? You may!	"So the wall was completed . . . in fifty-two days." (6:15)	Scripture found (7:5) read (8:3–7) explained (8:8) Lives changed (8:1–3, 9; 10:28–31)	Nation confronted and cleansed (13:10–30) Prayer
	CHAPTERS 1:1–2:10	*CHAPTERS 2:11–6:19*	*CHAPTERS 7–13*	
Location	Susa, Persia		Jerusalem in Judah	
Focus	Leadership of a man		Revival of a nation	
Subject	Burden	Project	Scriptures	Reforms
Difficulties	The King	Enemies	Tradition	Compromise
Victories	Release	Accomplishment	Obedience	Changes
Theme	Nehemiah's trust in the covenant-keeping God			
Key Verses	6:15–16; 8:8–10; 9:1–38			
Christ in Nehemiah	Suggested in Nehemiah, who leaves an exalted position to identify with the plight of his people and lead them into restoration; pictured in Nehemiah's prayerful dependence on God			

ESTHER

Who Wrote the Book?

The unknown author of the book of Esther was most likely a Jew very familiar with the royal Persian court. The detailed descriptions of court life and traditions, as well as the events that occurred in the book, point to an eyewitness author. Because his perspective was pro-Jewish, scholars believe he was a Jew writing for the remnant that had returned to Judah under Zerubbabel. Some have suggested Mordecai himself was the author, though the accolades for him found in the text suggest that another person, perhaps one of his younger contemporaries, was the author.

The book is named for the "star" of the story, a young Jewish girl named Hadassah who was taken from her guardian, Mordecai, and forced to compete for the affection of the king. This unlikely contestant for a beauty pageant was crowned queen of Persia and renamed Esther, meaning "star."

Where Are We?

The events in the book of Esther occurred from 483 BC to 473 BC, during the first half of the reign of King Xerxes, who chose Esther as his queen. During this time period, the first remnant of Jews who had returned to Judah were struggling to reestablish temple worship according to the Law of Moses. But Esther and Mordecai, along with many other Jews, had chosen not to make the trek back to Judah. They seemed content to stay in Susa, the capital city of Persia, in which the story is set.

The book was written no earlier than 470 BC and probably no later than 424 BC, during the reign of Xerxes' son Artaxerxes.

Why Is Esther so Important?

Esther is the only book in the Bible not to mention the name of God. But that is not to say that God was absent. His presence permeates much of the story, as though He were behind the scenes coordinating "coincidences" and circumstances to make His will happen.

Much like the book of Ruth, this book stands as one of the most skillfully written biblical books. Using eight feasts to systematically build and resolve suspense, the author constructed the story chiastically—using a Hebrew literary device in which events mirror each other inversely. Early listeners to the story would have recognized significant events and followed the rising tension with understanding.

Haman, the king's evil second-in-command, was a descendant of Agag, king of the Amalekites, who were ancient enemies of God's people (Numbers 24:7; 1 Samuel 15:8). He cast the lot, called "pur," in order to determine the day that the Jews would be exterminated (Esther 3:7–9). The feast of Purim, still celebrated by Jews today, commemorates the Jews' deliverance from Haman's plot (9:24–32).

What's the Big Idea?

While the primary purpose of the book of Esther was to relate the dramatic origins of the feast of Purim, a greater theme shines through the story. The sovereignty and faithfulness of God permeate each scene. Nothing is truly coincidental, the book of Esther says to us. God's sovereignty is best summarized in Mordecai's exhortation to Esther: "And who knows whether you have not attained royalty for such a time as this?" (Esther 4:14).

When events seemed out of control to Esther and Mordecai, when the king dictated ruin for their people, when evil was poised to triumph . . . God was at work. He worked through their dark days (Esther was taken to the harem [2:1–16]), their faithful obedience (Esther risked her life before the king [5:1–3]), and their victories (Esther revealed Haman's plot and the Jews' destruction of their enemies [7–9]). This message is clear: God is sovereign even when life doesn't make sense.

God is also the great Promise Keeper. Mordecai said to Esther: "If you remain silent at this time, relief and deliverance will arise for the Jews from another place and you and your father's house will perish" (Esther 4:14). Mordecai's words reflected his faith that God would honor His eternal covenant with Abraham and David.

How Do I Apply This?

Life can be hard. Difficult times happen, and pain cannot be avoided. When life doesn't make sense, do you turn to God or away from Him? Let the book of Esther encourage you that God is always present. Jesus called us "friends" (John 15:15), and the Spirit is our "Helper" (14:26). Trust and obey, as Esther did. And watch God silently weave all events for His glory . . . and for our good.

Esther

God's providence among His people during . . .

	Hard Times				**Happy Times**		
	King's Banquet	**Haman's Edict**	**Queen's Courage**	**God's Deliverance**	**Mordecai's Edict**	**Jews' Rejoicing**	**Shalom!**
	Honoring the kingdom Honoring the new queen		Urging of Mordecai Approaching the King	Mordecai honored Haman hanged		Enemies destroyed Feast established	
	CHAPTERS 1–2	*CHAPTER 3*	*CHAPTERS 4–5*	*CHAPTERS 6–7*	*CHAPTER 8*	*CHAPTER 9*	*CHAPTER 10*
Circumstances	Threat and trust				Deliverance and praise		
Feasts	of the king	of the queen			of the nation		
Dates	483 BC						473 BC
Theme	The sovereign accomplishment of God's purposes through ordinary people and apparent coincidences						
Key Verses	4:12–16; 10:3						
Christ in Esther	Pictured in Esther, who was an advocate for her people, even willing to die for them						

THE WISDOM BOOKS

The five Wisdom books—Job, Psalms, Proverbs, Ecclesiastes, and Song of Solomon—move away from the narrative and legal genres of the previous Old Testament books. Instead we find a collection of songs, prayers, proverbial statements, and most of all, poetry. Employing some of the most beautiful and vivid language in all of Scripture, these books tackle questions that penetrate the very core of life: how can we love our spouse well, how do we find meaning in life, and why do bad things happen to good people?

JOB

Who Wrote the Book?

The author of the book of Job is unknown. Several suggestions have been put forth as plausible authors: Job himself, who could have best recalled his own words; Elihu, the fourth friend who spoke toward the end of the story; various biblical writers and leaders; or many editors who compiled the material over the years. While there is no definitive answer, it was most likely an eyewitness who recorded the detailed and lengthy conversations found in the book. In Old Testament times, authors sometimes referred to themselves in the third person, so Job's authorship is a strong possibility.

Who was Job? This wealthy landowner and father is one of the best-known biblical heroes. But we know little more than that he was stripped of everything, without warning, and that his faith was severely tested.

Where Are We?

Though the text does not directly identify its setting, internal clues indicate that Job lived during the time of the patriarchs, approximately 2100 to 1900 BC. According to Job 42:16, Job lived an additional 140 years after his tragedies occurred, perhaps to around 210 years total. His long lifespan generally corresponds to that of Terah (Abraham's father), Abraham, Isaac, and Jacob. Also, Job's wealth was measured in livestock (Job 1:3; 42:12), as was Abraham's (Genesis 12:16). Like the patriarchs, Job used God's unique title "El Shaddai" (God Almighty). The book of Job does not mention the Mosaic Law; indeed, Job's daughters were equal heirs with his sons, and Job himself, though not a priest, offered sacrifices—things not possible under the Law (Leviticus 4:10; Numbers 27:8). Though we cannot be certain, Job may have lived during the time of Jacob or shortly thereafter.

Job lived in the land of Uz (Job 1:1), but no one really knows where Uz was located. Scholars believe it was outside of Canaan, near the desert because "the customs, vocabulary, and references to geography and natural history relate to northern Arabia."[1]

Why Is Job so Important?

The Israelites categorized Job within their wisdom literature. The book includes language from ancient legal proceedings, laments, and unique terms not found elsewhere in the Bible. In addition, the majority of Job is written in parallel lines which are indicative of poetry.

The book delves into issues near to the heart of every human who experiences suffering. The prologue provides a fascinating peek into the back story—why God allowed Satan to afflict Job with such pain and turmoil. Then, through a series of dialogues and monologues arranged in a pattern of threes, human wisdom attempts to explain the unexplainable, until finally God Himself speaks.

The final chapters of Job record God's masterful defense of His majesty and unique "otherness"—of God's eternal transcendence above creation—in contrast with Job's humble and ignorant mortality. "Where were you when I laid the foundation of the earth? / Tell Me, if you have understanding" (Job 38:4).

What's the Big Idea?

Job's plight of undeserved suffering compels us to ask the age-old question, "Why do bad things happen to good people?" The answer given to Job may or may not satisfy the reader. God allows pain for good reason, but He may never reveal those reasons.

Job did not reject God, but Job did challenge and accuse Him. The Almighty quieted Job decisively when He finally thundered His own perspective on the situation. God did not answer Job's question of

"Why?"—He instead overwhelmed Job and his friends with the truth of His majesty and sovereignty. Job came away with a deeper sense of God's power and splendor, trusting Him more:

> "I have heard of You by the hearing of the ear;
> But now my eye sees You;
> Therefore I retract,
> And I repent in dust and ashes." (Job 42:5–6)

How Do I Apply This?

Pain inevitably afflicts each one of us. Suffering is unavoidable in this life. Will your relationship with God be enough when trials come? Will you trust Him through your suffering? Read Job 38–42. Spend time with the Almighty. Pray for a stronger faith in the powerful Creator described in those chapters. Pray for a right perspective of Him so that you might see your situation through His eyes.

Instead of asking where God is in the midst of your pain, the book of Job affirms God's control and asks us, "Where are we in our pain? Are we trusting our Creator, even though we cannot understand our circumstances?"

JOB

	Introduction to the Suffering	Discussion of the Suffering				Correction in the Suffering		Submission under the Suffering	Restoration from the Suffering
	Scene 1 Job's purity and prosperity Scene 2 Satan's proposition and Yahweh's permission Scene 3 Satan's persecution and Job's patience Scene 4 Satan's persistence and Yahweh's permission Scene 5 Poverty and plagues	Words of Job (Eyes on Self) Curses birth Curses life	Words of Three Friends (Eyes on Humanity) Eliphaz ↔ Job → Zophar, Bildad		Eliphaz ↔ Job ↔ Bildad Job's monologue	Words of Elihu (Eyes on Yahweh) To Job To three friends To Job	Words of Yahweh (Emphasis on Sovereignty)	Job's admission Job's confession	Yahweh's anger with the three friends Yahweh's blessing on Job
			Eliphaz ↔ Job → Zophar, Bildad						
	CHAPTERS 1–2	*CHAPTER 3*	*CHAPTERS 4–14*	*CHAPTERS 15–21*	*CHAPTERS 22–31*	*CHAPTERS 32–37*	*CHAPTERS 38–41*	*CHAPTER 42:1–6*	*CHAPTER 42:7–17*
Key Sections	Historical	Theological / Philosophical				Logical	Revelational	Confessional	Historical
Key People	Job, Yahweh, and Satan	Job, Eliphaz, Bildad, and Zophar				Elihu	Yahweh	Job	Yahweh, Job, and the three friends
Key Sayings	"Have you considered My servant Job?" (1:8)	". . . then Job . . . Eliphaz . . . Bildad . . . Zophar answered"				God does "great things which we cannot comprehend." (37:5)	"Whatever is under the whole heaven is Mine." (41:11)	"Therefore I retract, / And I repent in dust and ashes." (42:6)	The LORD blessed the latter days of Job more than his beginning. (42:12)
Theme	God's sovereignty and humanity's struggle in the midst of suffering								
Key Verse	42:2								
Christ in Job	Job's cry for a mediator (9:33; 33:23–24) and his faith in a Redeemer (19:25–27) foreshadow the intercessory work of Christ.								

PSALMS

Who Wrote the Book?

Psalms, a collection of lyrical poems, is one of only two Old Testament books to identify itself as a composite work containing multiple authors (Proverbs is the other). Some psalms name their author in the first line or title. For example, Moses wrote Psalm 90. David was responsible for many of them, composing seventy-three psalms. Asaph wrote twelve; the descendants of Korah penned ten. Solomon wrote one or two, and Ethan and Heman the Ezrahites were responsible for two others. The remainder of the psalms do not contain information about their authors.

The book was originally titled *Tehillim*, which means "praise songs" in Hebrew. The English title of "Psalms" originated from the Septuagint's Greek title *Psalmoi*, also meaning "songs of praise."[1]

Where Are We?

Individual psalms were written as far back in history as Moses's time, through the time of David, Asaph, and Solomon, to the time of the Ezrahites who most likely lived after the Babylonian captivity, meaning the writing of the book spans one thousand years. Some of the psalms attributed to David have additional notations connecting them with documented events in his life (for example, Psalm 59 is linked with 1 Samuel 19:11; Psalm 56 is connected with 1 Samuel 21:10–15; Psalm 34 is associated with 1 Samuel 21:10–22:2; and Psalm 52 is linked with 1 Samuel 22:9).

The psalms are organized into five books or collections. They were probably collected gradually, as corporate worship forms developed along with temple worship. It is likely that by the time of Ezra, the books of the Psalter were organized into their final form. Each section concludes with a doxology, with the entire Psalter capped by Psalm 150, a grand doxology.

Why Is Psalms so Important?

The psalms comprised the ancient hymnal of God's people. The poetry was often set to music—but not always. The psalms express the emotion of the individual poet to God or about God. Different types of psalms were written to communicate different feelings and thoughts regarding a psalmist's situation.

Psalms of lament express the author's crying out to God in difficult circumstances. Psalms of praise, also called hymns, portray the author's offering of direct admiration to God. Thanksgiving psalms usually reflect the author's gratitude for a personal deliverance or provision from God. Pilgrim psalms include the title "a song of ascent" and were used on pilgrimages "going up" to Jerusalem for three annual festivals. Other types of psalms are referred to today as wisdom psalms, royal psalms (referring to Israel's king or Israel's Messiah), victory psalms, Law psalms, and songs of Zion.

The psalms include unique Hebrew terms. The word *Selah*, found seventy-one times, is most likely a musical notation added by worship leaders after the Israelites incorporated the psalm into public worship. Scholars do not know the meaning of *maskil*, found in thirteen psalms. Occasionally, a psalm appears with instructions for the song leader. For example, we see instructions such as "For the director of music" (occurring in fifty-five psalms [NIV]); "To the tune of 'Lilies'" (similar references found in Psalms 45, 60, 69, 80 NIV); "To the tune of 'The Doe of the Morning'" (Psalm 22 NIV); "To the tune of 'Do Not Destroy'" (Psalms 57–59, 75 NIV). These and others can refer to melodies used with the given psalm or perhaps to suggestions for liturgical use.

What's the Big Idea?

The book of Psalms expresses worship. Throughout its many pages, Psalms encourages its readers to praise God for who He is and what He has done. The Psalms illuminate the greatness of our God, affirm His faithfulness to us in times of trouble, and remind us of the absolute centrality of His Word. As the Psalms present a clear picture of God lovingly guiding His people, the responses of praise and worship to God are never far from the psalmists' pens. The portrayal of worship in the Psalms offers us glimpse after glimpse of hearts devoted to God, individuals repentant before Him, and lives changed through encounters with Him.

How Do I Apply This?

Read Psalm 1, then Psalm 150. Thank God for allowing you to express your deepest emotions to Him. If you are hurting, use Psalm 13 as a guide and write your own lament to God. If you are rejoicing, meditate on Psalm 30 and echo the praise found there. No matter your circumstance, the psalms contain a corresponding word that will help you share your heart with the Lord.

Psalms

1490 BC DAYS OF MOSES — 444 BC DAYS OF EZRA

	Book One	Book Two	Book Three	Book Four	Book Five
	41 Psalms	31 Psalms	17 Psalms	17 Psalms	44 Psalms
	HUMANITY	DELIVERANCE	SANCTUARY	REIGN OF GOD	WORD OF GOD
	PSALMS 1–41	*PSALMS 42–72*	*PSALMS 73–89*	*PSALMS 90–106*	*PSALMS 107–150*
Analogy	Genesis	Exodus	Leviticus	Numbers	Deuteronomy
Content	Personal	Devotional	Liturgical, Historical	General	Prophetical, Natural
Doxology	Psalm 41:13	Psalm 72:18–19	Psalm 89:52	Psalm 106:48	Psalm 150
Theme	We worship God for who He is and what He has done.				
Key Verse	19:14				
Christ in Psalms	Jesus Christ is anticipated, portrayed, and prophesied in such images as the coming King, the Redeemer, the loving Shepherd, and the Righteous Sufferer.				

PROVERBS

Who Wrote the Book?

Proverbs, like Psalms, names multiple individuals as the authors of its various sections. Solomon was uniquely qualified to serve as the principal author for this book of wise sayings. First Kings 3:5–9 recounts Solomon asking God for wisdom in his reign over Israel, a request God eventually granted (1 Kings 4:29–31). In fact, Solomon identified himself as the source of most of the book. His name appears at the beginning of three distinct sections—Proverbs 1:1, 10:1, and 25:1—covering almost all of the first twenty-nine chapters of the book.

A short section consisting of Proverbs 22:17–24:34 expresses "the words of the wise" (Proverbs 22:17), which Solomon may have compiled from various sources. Evidence that Solomon drew on multiple sources appears in Proverbs 24:23, where Solomon used the plural noun for "wise" (also translated *sages*) to describe the authors of this section. Also, due to the book's similarities with Mesopotamian and Egyptian collections of proverbs such as "The Instruction of Amenemope," it's possible that God inspired Solomon to record this section based on wise sayings he had been exposed to throughout his life.[1]

The final two chapters identify Agur (30:1) and Lemuel (31:1) as their authors, though the identities of these men remain mysterious in history.

Where Are We?

The composition of Proverbs remains one of the most difficult questions about the book. Its strong association with Solomon means most of its contents were completed prior to his death in 931 BC. Clearly the book stayed in the southern kingdom of Judah, as Hezekiah's men compiled more of Solomon's proverbs in Proverbs 25–29. This indicates that the book was likely in its final form sometime before the end of Hezekiah's reign in 686 BC.

Why Is Proverbs so Important?

Proverbs accomplishes something no other biblical book does: it simply compiles numerous short instructions for living an effective life on earth. While other books articulate profound theological truths, lengthy narratives of triumph and failure, or prophetic preaching to a disobedient people, Proverbs concerns itself completely with instructing people in the path of wisdom. The writers of the book recognized the varied circumstances of a person's life and provided principles to apply in a variety of situations rather than instructions to follow in only a few specific instances.

What's the Big Idea?

Proverbs states its theme explicitly very early in the book: "The fear of the Lord is the beginning of knowledge" (Proverbs 1:7). The fear of the Lord refers to our viewing Him with the respect He deserves. It means living our lives in light of what we know of Him, holding Him in the highest estimation, and depending on Him with humble trust. Only then, Proverbs teaches, will we discover knowledge and wisdom (see also 9:10).

In writing the Proverbs, Solomon hoped that his readers would attain practical righteousness in all things and that we would do this by living our lives under the authority and direction of God. He specifically explained the book's purpose in 1:2–6, focusing on imparting understanding that would impact every facet of our lives. Much of the book emphasizes listening to others so that we might learn from them and apply the combined knowledge of those who have gone before us—such as parents and elders—to the unique circumstances of our own lives (1:5, 8). Wisdom then involves appropriating a measure of humility, first before God and then before others. If instead, we decide to speak rashly rather than listen attentively . . . well, Proverbs deals with that too (12:15; 13:3).

How Do I Apply This?

Read it! Then live it! Proverbs contains some of the most applicable nuggets of truth in all of the Bible. Most of the proverbs are pithy statements brimming over with imagery from the real world. This approach allows us to see very clearly how any particular proverb might be applied to any number of everyday situations we encounter—from getting out of bed in the morning to building a strong foundation in our relationships with others. Proverbs reminds us that God concerns Himself not just with the big, cataclysmic events of life but even those mundane, "invisible" moments in our lives as well.

Are you following God, even in those seemingly "small" circumstances? Allow Proverbs to refocus your attention on all the hidden moments of your life.

PROVERBS

	Prologue to Wise Living The fear of the LORD is the beginning of knowledge. (1:7) *CHAPTERS 1–9*	**Principles for Wise Living** The fear of the LORD is the instruction for wisdom, / And before honor comes humility. (15:33) *CHAPTERS 10:1–31:9*	**Personification of Wise Living** Charm is deceitful and beauty is vain, / But a woman who fears the LORD, she shall be praised. (31:30) *CHAPTER 31:10–31*
Emphasis	Wisdom especially for youth	Wisdom for all	
Framework	Subjects and statements	People and problems	Counseling and correction
Style	A book filled with short statements that declare a profound truth providing wisdom for life		
Theme	"The fear of the LORD is the beginning of wisdom" (9:10).		
Key Verse	9:10		
Christ in Proverbs	Wisdom is incarnate in Christ "in whom are hidden all the treasures of wisdom and knowledge" (1 Corinthians 1:24, 30; Colossians 2:3).		

ECCLESIASTES

Who Wrote the Book?

The title "Ecclesiastes" comes from a Greek word indicating a person who calls an assembly, so it makes sense that the author identified himself in Ecclesiastes 1:1 by the Hebrew word *qoheleth*, translated as "Preacher." Despite leaving only this rather mysterious name to indicate his identity, evidence in the book, along with most Jewish and Christian tradition, suggests that King Solomon authored Ecclesiastes.

The Preacher went on to call himself "the son of David, king in Jerusalem," one who has increased in "wisdom more than all who were over Jerusalem before me," and one who has collected many proverbs (Ecclesiastes 1:1, 16; 12:9). Solomon followed David on the throne in Jerusalem as the only Davidic son to rule over all Israel from that city (1:12). He was the wisest man in the world during his time (1 Kings 4:29–30) and wrote most of the book of Proverbs (Proverbs 1:1; 10:1; 25:1). Therefore, we can safely identify Solomon as the *qoheleth* of the opening verse.

Where Are We?

With Solomon as the author of the book, we know it had to have been written sometime before his death in 931 BC. The content of Ecclesiastes reflects someone looking back on a life that was long on experience but short on lasting rewards. As king, he had the opportunity and resources to pursue the rewards of wisdom, pleasure, and work in and of themselves. Yet the world-weary tone of the writing suggests that late in life, he looked back on his folly with regret, pointing us to a better, simpler life lived in light of God's direction (Ecclesiastes 12:13–14).

Why Is Ecclesiastes so Important?

Ecclesiastes presents us a naturalistic vision of life—one that sees life through distinctively human eyes—but ultimately recognizes the rule and reign of God in the world. This more humanistic quality has made the book especially popular among younger audiences today, men and women who have seen more than their fair share of pain and instability in life but who still cling to their hope in God.

What's the Big Idea?

Ecclesiastes, like much of life, represents a journey from one point to another. Solomon articulated his starting point early in the book: "Vanity of vanities! All is vanity" (Ecclesiastes 1:2), indicating the utter futility and meaninglessness of life as he saw it. Nothing made sense to him because he had already tried any number of remedies—pleasure, work, and intellect—to alleviate his sense of feeling lost in the world.

However, even in the writer's desperate search for meaning and significance in life, God remained present. For instance, we read that God provides food, drink, and work (2:24); both the sinner and the righteous person live in God's sight (2:26); God's deeds are eternal (3:14); and God empowers people to enjoy His provision (5:19). Ultimately, the great truth of Ecclesiastes lies in the acknowledgment of God's ever-present hand on our lives. Even when injustice and uncertainty threaten to overwhelm us, we can trust Him and follow after Him (12:13–14).

How Do I Apply This?

We all desire meaning in life. Often that search takes us along winding, up-and-down paths filled with bursts of satisfaction that shine bright for a time but eventually fade. In one sense, it's satisfying to see that experience echoed throughout Ecclesiastes. An appreciation for our common humanity emerges from reading its pages. We relate to the journey of Solomon because, for so many of us, it is our own. When we attempt to find meaning in the pursuit of pleasure, the commitment to a job, or through plumbing intellectual depths, we all eventually find in each of these pursuits a dead end.

Ecclesiastes shows us a man who lived through this process and came out on the other side with a wiser, more seasoned perspective. When we're surrounded by the temptation to proclaim life's ultimate emptiness, we can find in Ecclesiastes a vision tempered by experience and ultimately seen through divinely colored lenses. Life is destined to remain unsatisfying apart from our recognition of God's intervention. It only remains to be seen whether or not we will place our trust in His sure and able hands.

Have you struggled with misplaced pursuits in life? Does your life lack the meaning and purpose you desire? Hear the words of Solomon that they might encourage you to place your trust solely in the Lord.

Ecclesiastes

	Introduction	Investigation and Discoveries ***I set my mind to seek and explore by wisdom. (1:13)***		Admonition	Conclusion
	Writer Theme Questions and illustrations	PERSONAL PURSUITS Knowledge Amusements Possessions Madness and folly Labor Philosophy Riches V A N I T Y	CONCLUSIONS **Without God's help:** Humans cannot discover what is good for them to do. **Without God's revelation:** Humans do not know what will come after them.	A warning to the young A picture of old age A final admission	THE END OF THE SEARCH Fear God! Obey Him! Someday you will face Him!
	CHAPTER 1:1–11	*CHAPTERS 1:12–6:12*	*CHAPTERS 7:1–11:6*	*CHAPTERS 11:7–12:8*	*CHAPTERS 12:9–14*
Search	Nature	Philosophy Materialism	Fatalism Relationships	Theology	
Style	Proverbial	Personal		Poetical	
Theme	The meaninglessness of life apart from God				
Key Verses	2:11; 12:13–14				
Christ in Ecclesiastes	The "one Shepherd" (12:11) who offers abundant life				

SONG OF SOLOMON

Who Wrote the Book?

Song of Solomon takes its title from the first verse of the book, which mentions who the song comes from: "The Song of Songs, which is Solomon's" (Song of Solomon 1:1). The original Hebrew version of the book took its title from the book's first two words, *shiyr hashiyrim*, usually translated as "the song of songs." This latter title remained in Greek and Latin Bible translations in later centuries. The repetition of the word *song* indicates that the writer considered this "the greatest of all songs."[1] We find a similar construction in other famous biblical phrases: Lord of Lords, King of Kings, and Holy of Holies, to name a few.

The title of the book eventually took on King Solomon's name because of the mention of his name throughout the book (1:5; 3:7, 9, 11; 8:11–12). This title change also supports the traditional view of Solomon as the author of the book. While numerous critics in the last two centuries have disputed Solomon's authorship, the internal evidence seems to support it, not only because of the appearances of Solomon's name but because of evidence of his royal advantage (3:6–11) and his numerous wives and concubines (6:8).

Where Are We?

Solomon wrote the book during his reign as king of Israel, meaning he composed it sometime between 971 and 931 BC. Scholars who hold to Solomon's authorship tend to agree that the song was written early in his reign, not merely because of the youthful exuberance of the poetry but because his harem of 140 women, mentioned in 6:8, is relatively low in number compared to the final tally of 1,000 (1 Kings 11:3). Also, the author mentioned place names from both the north and the south of the country, including Lebanon and Egypt, reminding us of the relative peace and good relations among these nations early in Solomon's reign.

Why Is Song of Solomon so Important?

This book remains singular within the Old Testament for at least two reasons: its character as a single poem and its subject matter, particularly the frank discussion of love between a married couple. The Song of Solomon's willingness to broach the topic of physical love within marriage has made many of its readers throughout history uncomfortable, so much so that Rabbi Aqiba had to vigorously defend the book's place in the Jewish canon even as late as AD 90 at the Council of Jamnia.[2] But as a testament to the beauty of the marriage relationship in its fullness, Song of Solomon stands out with its uniquely detailed vision of this beautiful reality.

What's the Big Idea?

The fullness of the union that takes place at marriage is described in some of the most splendid poetic language in the entire Bible. In a world where so many speak of God's special gifts with coldly clinical or apathetic statistical language, the passion of Solomon's poetry refreshes a world thirsty for the truth about marriage. Solomon began his rendering of this relationship with the two lovers in courtship longing for affection while expressing their love for one another (Song of Solomon 1:1–3:5). Eventually, they come together in marriage, the groom extolling his bride's beauty before they consummate their relationship (3:6–5:1). Finally, she struggles with the fear of separation, while he reassures his bride of his affections for her (5:2–8:14). All of this reinforces the theme of the goodness of marriage. Some suggest the book also pictures in a more general way Christ's love for His bride, the church.

How Do I Apply This?

From courtship to marriage to the assurance of love, Song of Solomon poetically presents a broad range of events and feelings in the days leading up to and during marriage, offering encouragement toward an enduring love amid the petty jealousies and fears sure to threaten even the strongest of relationships. We should heed the Song's sublime words by continuing to value marriage as one of the bedrocks of society, appreciating the goodness and the beauty borne out of the union of two people in holy matrimony.

Would you consider your marriage a sign of God's goodness and beauty working in your life, or has it become something less than that over time? Song of Solomon reminds us that both marriage and the physical union that follows originate in God; we should therefore consider each of them as evidence of His grace working itself out in the world.

Song of Solomon

	The Courtship	The Wedding	The Maturing Marriage		
	CHAPTERS 1:2–3:5	*CHAPTERS 3:6–5:1*	*CHAPTERS 5:2–8:14*		
Emphasis	Bride muses about her beloved	Groom speaks tenderly to his bride	Wife longs for and describes her loving husband	Husband speaks of his wife in intimate terms	Both partners declare a permanent seal on their love
Chief Speaker	The Bride ("Darling")	The Groom ("Beloved")	Wife ("Darling")	Husband ("Beloved")	Duet
Theme	The joy and intimacy of love within the committed marriage relationship				
Key Verse	8:7				
Christ in Song of Solomon	Foreshadows the bridegroom relationship of Christ with His church				

THE MAJOR PROPHETS

The books of the Major Prophets—Isaiah, Jeremiah, Lamentations, Ezekiel, and Daniel—are named as such not for their importance in comparison to the Minor Prophets but because of their longer length. These books serve two main functions: foretelling and "forth-telling." Foretelling involves predicting certain events in both the near and the distant future, while forth-telling involves bringing forth the truth about God's ways into the present lives of a sinful people. While they are usually thought of as foretellers of judgment and restoration, the major prophets actually spent the bulk of their words on forth-telling—calling the people back to faithfulness.

ISAIAH

Who Wrote the Book?

As is the case with nearly all the books of "the prophets," the book of Isaiah takes its name from its writer. Isaiah was married to a prophetess who bore him at least two sons (Isaiah 7:3; 8:3). He prophesied under the reign of four Judean kings—Uzziah, Jotham, Ahaz, and Hezekiah (1:1)—and he likely met his death under a fifth, the evil King Manasseh. Christian tradition as early as the second century identifies Isaiah as one of the prophets whose death is described in Hebrews 11:37, specifically the prophet who was "sawn in two."[1] Isaiah likely lived in Jerusalem, given the book's concern with the city (Isaiah 1:1) and his close proximity to at least two significant kings during the period of his prophecy (7:3; 38:1).

Much of scholarship for the past two centuries has assigned multiple writers to Isaiah, dividing the book into three sections: 1–39, 40–55, and 56–66. However, these divisions come out of a scholarly denial of predictive prophecy. This position not only limits the power of God to communicate with His people but also ignores the wide variety of specific, predictive claims about Jesus Christ scattered throughout the book.

Where Are We?

Isaiah prophesied from 739–681 BC to a nation that had turned a deaf ear to the Lord. Instead of serving Him with humility and offering love to their neighbors, the nation of Judah offered meaningless sacrifices in God's temple at Jerusalem and committed injustices throughout the nation. The people of Judah turned their backs on God and alienated themselves from Him, which created the need for Isaiah's pronouncements of judgment—declarations made in the hope that God's chosen people would return to Him.

Why Is Isaiah so Important?

The book of Isaiah provides us with the most comprehensive prophetic picture of Jesus Christ in the entire Old Testament. It includes the full scope of His life: the announcement of His coming (Isaiah 40:3–5), His virgin birth (7:14), His proclamation of the good news (61:1), His sacrificial death (52:13–53:12), and His return to claim His own (60:2–3). Because of these and numerous other christological texts in Isaiah, the book stands as a testament of hope in the Lord, the One who saves His people from themselves.

What's the Big Idea?

Isaiah's overall theme receives its clearest statement in chapter 12: "Behold, God is my salvation, / I will trust and not be afraid" (Isaiah 12:2). This echoes the meaning of Isaiah's name, which means the "salvation of Yahweh."[2] Having read the book, one might wonder about the strong presence of judgment that runs through the first thirty-nine chapters when the theme is salvation. How can the two coexist? The presence of judgment indicates its necessity for salvation to occur. Before we can have salvation, we must have a need for it!

So the bulk of those early chapters in Isaiah detail judgments against the people who have turned their backs on the Lord, showing us that those who persist in their rebellion will receive judgment. On the other hand, we also see God's faithfulness to His promise. He will preserve a small remnant of faithful believers, those who will continue on into the glorious renewed world He has prepared for His children in the end times (65:17–66:24).

How Do I Apply This?

Because of its scope, Isaiah contains one of the clearest expressions of the gospel in all the Old Testament. Even from the first chapter, it is clear that the people have turned away from God and failed in their responsibilities as His children (Isaiah 1:2–17). Yet God miraculously holds out hope to this unrepentant people, offering cleansing of sins and the blessing that comes with faith and obedience in Him (1:18–20). Salvation lies only in God—the only question is whether or not we will accept His offer.

In addition to its gospel message, the book of Isaiah clearly articulates the sins of God's people—dealing with others unjustly which resulted in their offering hypocritical sacrifices to God. Do you see anything in your own life that might fall under Isaiah's critique of injustice—treating family, colleagues, or even strangers with unkindness or even disdain? Isaiah's message is also a call for believers to come back to purity in our love for God and for our neighbors (Luke 10:26–28).

Isaiah

	The Judgment of God	The Deliverance of God		
		THE SUPREMACY OF THE LORD	THE SERVANT OF THE LORD Servant Songs: 42:1–9 49:1–13 50:4–11 52:13–53:12	THE FUTURE PLAN OF THE LORD
	CHAPTERS 1–39	*CHAPTERS 40–48*	*CHAPTERS 49–53*	*CHAPTERS 54–66*
Emphasis	The law and judgment for disobedience	God's grace and deliverance Comfort . . .	Promise . . .	Hope . . .
"Bible within Bible"	Old Testament	New Testament		
Theme	The justice and mercy of God			
Key Verses	2:3–5; 6:1–3; 53:1–12			
Christ in Isaiah	His first and second advents are prophesied throughout the book (child of a virgin in 7:14, the shoot from the stem of Jesse in chapter 11, the Suffering Servant in chapter 53).			

JEREMIAH

Who Wrote the Book?

The son of a priest from the small town of Anathoth in Judah, the prophet Jeremiah dictated prophecies from the Lord to his secretary, Baruch. Because of Jeremiah's lineage, he would have been raised a priest, though no record of his priestly service exists. Instead, God chose this man of undeniable courage to speak to the people of Judah on the Lord's behalf—even though they would not listen.

Jeremiah was nearly twenty years old when he began to prophesy, and he continued in that office for the rest of his adult life, some forty years or more. Because his message held little weight with the people, Jeremiah's prophecies reveal a substantial amount of emotional depth—often sorrow over the plight of God's people or his own troubles (Jeremiah 12:1–4; 15:10).

Where Are We?

Jeremiah's ministry began in 627 BC and ended sometime around 582 BC with his prophecy to the Jews who fled to Egypt (Jeremiah 44:1). For the majority of this time, Jeremiah based his ministry out of Jerusalem. The southern kingdom of Judah fell during Jeremiah's prophetic ministry (586 BC), having been threatened for many years by outside powers—first Assyria and Egypt and then by their eventual conquerors, Babylon.

Jeremiah found himself addressing a nation hurtling headlong toward judgment from God. The Israelites may have feared the future as the outside powers drew near, but rather than respond with humility and repentance, the people of Judah primarily lived as islands unto themselves, disregarding both the Lord's commandments and the increasing danger that resulted from their disobedience.

Why Is Jeremiah so Important?

The prophecies of Jeremiah offer us a unique insight into the mind and heart of one of God's faithful servants. The book includes numerous personal statements of emotional engagement, painting Jeremiah not merely as a prophet brought on the scene to deliver God's message but also as a red-blooded human being who felt compassion for his people, desired judgment for evildoers, and was concerned about his own safety as well.

Significantly, the book of Jeremiah also provides us the clearest glimpse of the new covenant God intended to make with His people once Christ came to earth. This new covenant would be the means of restoration for God's people, as He would put His law within them, writing it on hearts of flesh rather than on tablets of stone. Rather than fostering our relationship with God through a fixed location like a temple, He promised through Jeremiah that His people would know Him directly, a knowledge that comes through the person of His Son, Jesus Christ (Jeremiah 31:31–34; see also Hebrews 8:6).

What's the Big Idea?

Because Jeremiah prophesied in the final years of Judah before God's people were exiled to Babylon, it makes sense that the book's overarching theme is judgment. Indeed, the first forty-five chapters focus primarily on the judgment coming to Judah because of its disbelief and disobedience. However, an element of grace is also present in these events. The fall of Jerusalem comes nearly nine hundred years after the original covenant between God and the Israelites in the Sinai desert (Exodus 24:1–18). Such an extended period of time witnesses to God's great patience and mercy, allowing His people the opportunity to turn from their sinful ways—a lifestyle they began not long after they struck the original covenant with God (32:1–35).

How Do I Apply This?

Seeing God's patience with His people in the Old Testament reminds us that God has always been and continues to be merciful. That His chosen people routinely ignored the covenant they made with Him for the better part of a millennia without immediate death and destruction should give us hope in our own struggles with living well for God. Though we fail Him, He is patient with us, working in us to bring about the best for our lives.

But the book of Jeremiah also reminds us that an end will certainly come, a truth that should spur us to follow after God wholeheartedly. Will you follow Him?

Jeremiah

	Judah's Sin and Judgment	Prophecies against the Nations	A Sobering Ending
	Jeremiah's call Idolatry Corrupt leadership Moral compromise Exhortations to Judah Promises of restoration (30–33) Fall of Jerusalem and aftermath (39–45)	Egypt Philistia Moab Ammon Edom Damascus Kedar & Hazor Elam Babylon	Jerusalem in ruins
	CHAPTERS 1–45	*CHAPTERS 46–51*	*CHAPTER 52*
Theme	Judgment is coming; repent!		
Key Verses	7:23–24; 8:11–12, 21; 9:23–24; 31:1–40		
Christ in Jeremiah	The fountain of living waters (2:13); the righteous Branch, Coming Shepherd, the LORD our righteousness (23:4–6); the New Covenant (31:31); Redeemer (50:34)		

LAMENTATIONS

Who Wrote the Book?

While the author of Lamentations remains nameless within the book, strong evidence from both inside and outside the text points to the prophet Jeremiah as the author. Both Jewish and Christian tradition ascribe authorship to Jeremiah, and the Septuagint—the Greek translation of the Old Testament—even adds a note asserting Jeremiah as the writer of the book. In addition, when the early Christian church father Jerome translated the Bible into Latin, he added a note claiming Jeremiah as the author of Lamentations.

The original name of the book in Hebrew, *ekah*, can be translated "Alas!" or "How," giving the sense of weeping or lamenting over some sad event.[1] Later readers and translators substituted in the title "Lamentations" because of its clearer and more evocative meaning. It's this idea of lamenting that, for many, links Jeremiah to the book. Not only does the author of the book witness the results of the recent destruction of Jerusalem, he seems to have witnessed the invasion itself (Lamentations 1:13–15). Jeremiah was present for both events.

Where Are We?

"How lonely sits the city / That was full of people!" (Lamentations 1:1), so goes the beginning of Lamentations. The city in question was none other than Jerusalem. Jeremiah walked through the streets and alleys of the Holy City and saw nothing but pain, suffering, and destruction in the wake of the Babylonian invasion of 586 BC. It also makes sense to date the book as close to the invasion as possible, meaning late 586 BC or early 585 BC, due to the raw emotion Jeremiah expresses throughout its pages

Why Is Lamentations so Important?

Like the book of Job, Lamentations pictures a man of God puzzling over the results of evil and suffering in the world. However, while Job dealt with unexplained evil, Jeremiah lamented a tragedy entirely of Jerusalem's making. The people of this once great city experienced the judgment of the holy God, and the results were devastating. But at the heart of this book, at the center of this lament over the effects of sin in the world, sit a few verses devoted to hope in the Lord (Lamentations 3:22–25). This statement of faith standing strong in the midst of the surrounding darkness shines as a beacon to all those suffering under the consequences of their own sin and disobedience.

What's the Big Idea?

As the verses of Lamentations accumulate, readers cannot help but wonder how many different ways Jeremiah could describe the desolation of the once proud city of Jerusalem. Children begged food from their mothers (Lamentations 2:12), young men and women were cut down by swords (2:21), and formerly compassionate mothers used their children for food (4:10). Even the city's roads mourned over its condition (1:4)! Jeremiah could not help but acknowledge the abject state of this city, piled with rubble.

The pain so evident in Jeremiah's reaction to this devastation clearly communicates the significance of the terrible condition in Jerusalem. Speaking in the first person, Jeremiah pictured himself captured in a besieged city, without anyone to hear his prayers, and as a target for the arrows of the enemy (3:7–8, 12). Yet even in this seemingly hopeless situation, he somehow found hope in the Lord (3:21–24).

How Do I Apply This?

Lamentations reminds us of the importance not only of mourning over our sin but of asking the Lord for His forgiveness when we fail Him. Much of Jeremiah's poetry concerns itself with the fallen bricks and cracking mortar of the overrun city. Do you see any of that destroyed city in your own life? Are you mourning over the sin that's brought you to this point? Do you feel overrun by an alien power; are you in need of some hope from the Lord? Turn to Lamentations 3:17–26, where you'll find someone aware of sin's consequences and saddened by the results but who has placed his hope and his trust in the Lord.

Lamentations

	Jerusalem's Desolation *CHAPTER 1*	The Lord's Anger *CHAPTER 2*	Jeremiah's Grief *CHAPTER 3*	The Lord's Anger *CHAPTER 4*	Jeremiah's Prayer *CHAPTER 5*
Underlying Emotion	Lonely, groaning	Angry, exhorting	Broken, weeping	Desperate, anguished	Weary, pleading
Short Prayers	1:20–22 *"See us!"*	2:20–22 *"Look at us!"*	3:55–66 *"Judge them!"*	4:20 *"Avenge us!"*	5:21 *"Restore us!"*
Theme	Mourning over sin; the severity of God's judgment; hope in His mercy				
Key Verses	1:1, 5	2:14, 17	3:16–24	4:11–12	5:5, 19–22
Christ in Lamentations	Jesus, like Jeremiah, wept over the sins of Jerusalem (Matthew 23:27–38; Luke 13:34–35).				

EZEKIEL

Who Wrote the Book?

The book of Ezekiel takes its title from the priest of the same name, son to a man named Buzi. Ezekiel's priestly lineage shines through in his prophetic ministry; he often concerned himself with topics such as the temple, the priesthood, the glory of the Lord, and the sacrificial system.

Ezekiel 1:1 tells us that the prophecy began "in the thirtieth year." Scholars usually consider this a reference to Ezekiel's age, making him about the same age as Daniel, who was exiled to Babylon nearly a decade earlier. Like many priests of Israel, Ezekiel was married. But when his wife died during his prophetic ministry, God prevented Ezekiel from mourning her in public as a sign of Judah's lack of concern for the things of God (Ezekiel 24:16–24).

Where Are We?

Ezekiel lived among the Jewish exiles in Babylon at a settlement along the river Chebar called Tel-abib (Ezekiel 3:15), less than one hundred miles south of Babylon. The invading Babylonians brought about ten thousand Jews to the village in 597 BC, including Ezekiel and the last king of Judah, Jehoiachin (2 Kings 24:8–14).

Ezekiel's prophecy began a mere five years into his time at Tel-abib (Ezekiel 1:2), and he continued to prophesy among the people for at least twenty-two years (29:17). Because he spoke to a people whom God had exiled due to their continued rebellion against Him, a majority of Ezekiel's message communicates judgment for sins committed (1:1–32:32). However, like all the prophets, he also provided his people, now without a land of their own, some hope for the future (33:1–48:35).

Why Is Ezekiel so Important?

The book of Ezekiel pronounces judgment on both Israel and surrounding nations, but it also provides a vision of the future millennial kingdom that complements and adds to the vision of other Old and New Testament texts. Not only does the book present a striking picture of the resurrection and restoration of God's people (Ezekiel 37), it also offers readers a picture of the reconstructed temple in Jerusalem, complete with the return of God's glory to His dwelling place (40:1–48:35). This latter section of Ezekiel's prophecy looks forward to the people's worship after Christ's return in the end times, when He will rule Israel and the nations from His throne in Jerusalem during His thousand year reign.

What's the Big Idea?

God didn't exile the Israelites primarily to punish them. God never has been nor is He now interested in punishment for punishment's sake. Rather, He intended the punishment or judgment in Ezekiel's day as a means to an end—to bring His people to a state of repentance and humility before the one true God. They had lived for so long in sin and rebellion, confident in their own strength and that of the neighboring nations, that they needed God to remind them of His holy nature and their humble identity in a most dramatic way. After centuries of warnings, prophetic messages, and invasions, God decided that more significant action was required—He had to remove the people from their promised land.

How Do I Apply This?

Ezekiel's entire prophetic ministry centered around the small exiled community at Tel-abib, a people uprooted from their homes and livelihoods living out their days in a foreign land. Can you imagine the feelings of disorientation and confusion that accompanied these people? Even though many of the exiles were directly engaged in the sinful behavior that led to God's judgment, that would not prevent them from wondering why all this was happening to them.

We sometimes find ourselves in that predicament as well, asking "Why, Lord?" and waiting in silence for the answer. The exiles had to wait five years for God to send Ezekiel, and when God did, His prophet had a message that the people likely didn't want to hear: God is the Lord of heaven and earth, and the judgment the people were experiencing was a result of their own sin.

The book of Ezekiel reminds us to seek out the Lord in those dark times when we feel lost, to examine our own lives, and to align ourselves with the one true God. Will you consider doing so today?

EZEKIEL

	About the Prophet	Judgment on Judah	Judgment on the Nations	Restoration of God's People
	EZEKIEL'S CALL AND COMMISSION God's hand on him God's word in him God's message through him	GOD'S GLORY DEPARTS	ALL NATIONS ANSWER TO GOD	GOD'S GLORY RETURNS
	CHAPTERS 1–3	*CHAPTERS 4–24*	*CHAPTERS 25–32*	*CHAPTERS 33–48*
Theme	God will be known through His judgment and restoration; God is sovereign over heaven and earth.			
Key Verse	39:28			
Christ in Ezekiel	The tender twig that becomes a stately cedar (17:22–24); the caring shepherd (chapter 34)			

DANIEL

Who Wrote the Book?

Named after its writer, Daniel's book is a product of his time in Babylon as a Jewish exile from Israel. While still a young man, Daniel travelled to Babylon with a group of young Israelite nobles, men of promise whom the conquering power felt could be of use in service (Daniel 1:3–4). Once Daniel arrived, the leadership in Babylon renamed him Belteshazzar in an effort to more closely identify him with his new home (1:7). Daniel lived there throughout the Jews' seventy-year captivity (1:21; 9:2), eventually rising to become one of only three administrators over the provincial governors throughout the kingdom (6:1).

Daniel recorded his experiences and prophecies for the Jewish exiles during his time in the Babylonian capital, where his service to the king gave him privileged access to the highest levels of society. His faithful service to the Lord in a land and culture not his own makes him unique among almost all the people of Scripture—Daniel stands as one of the only major figures in the Bible to produce a completely positive record of his actions.

Where Are We?

The Babylonians exiled the group containing Daniel and his three friends—best known by their Babylonian names, Shadrach, Meshach, and Abed-nego—to the cultural center of the their empire, the city of Babylon, in 605 BC. This move was part of the first of three deportations (605, 597, and 586 BC) carried out by the Babylonians in Israel after they subdued Jerusalem and the unfaithful King Jehoiakim

(2 Kings 23:36–24:2). The teenaged Daniel found himself in the midst of a strongly polytheistic religious culture, meaning he had ample opportunities to fall into error. However, he stood firm in his faith among the Babylonian people on several significant matters—including dietary regulations and worship practices (Daniel 1:8–16; 6:6–12).

Why Is Daniel so Important?

Daniel is one of the few Bible books that takes place during a period of judgment (many books foretell it and a few look back on it) and in a foreign nation. Whether it's in the contrast between the culture's idol worship and Daniel's faithful purity or in the account of the arrogant Nebuchadnezzar and his humbling encounter with God, the pagan backdrop in Daniel makes the Lord's power shine through in a magnificent and majestic way that stands out in Scripture. The book of Daniel makes it clear that the true God is the supreme ruler over heaven and earth (Daniel 4:17), even when all seems lost and the consequences of sin seem overwhelming.

What's the Big Idea?

The book of Daniel stands as a unique mix in the Old Testament, for while it begins with history, it makes a strong transition at chapter 7, where it contains visions of future events significant to the Jews. In particular, Daniel 9:24–27 gives a meticulous timeline of when Israel's Messiah would appear and the events that would follow.

In both the historical and the prophetic sections, Daniel presents a strong case for the absolute sovereignty of God, even over a multiplicity of self-absorbed foreign powers. This theme of sovereignty occurs on numerous occasions, including Daniel's deliverance from the lions' den, his friends' rescue from the fiery furnace, and the future arrival of the Ancient of Days to save His people from the forces of evil (Daniel 3:23–30; 6:19–23; 7:9–22).

How Do I Apply This?

Daniel and his God-fearing friends were forced to live in Babylon, far from home and far from the land their Lord had promised them. Later in the book, Daniel prophesied of terrible trials still to come in the Promised Land (Daniel 11:31). Whatever the trial was, though, it was always the result of sin.

Have you ever endured the weight or consequences of sin and felt as though God had left you behind, that He had stranded you in a world far from the comforts associated with home? The book of Daniel paints a portrait of how to serve God faithfully in the middle of such a world and how to persevere in hope even with no immediate solutions to the problems that get us down.

DANIEL

	Biographical Section Daniel Interprets Others' Dreams		Prophetical Section Angel Interprets Daniel's Dreams	
	MAIN EMPHASIS: DANIEL THE PROPHET Introduction and setting (1) Nebuchadnezzar's apocalyptic dream (2) Historical narratives (political and personal) (3–6)		MAIN EMPHASIS: THE PROPHECIES OF DANIEL Daniel's foundational vision (7) Prophetic visions (near and far) (8–12)	
	CHAPTERS *1–6*		*CHAPTERS* *7–12*	
	POLITICAL POWERS **Babylonian Rule** Nebuchadnezzar Belshazzar	. . . IN DANIEL'S DAY **Medo-Persian Rule** Darius Cyrus	**Grecian Rule** Alexander the Great Four generals	. . . AND AFTERWARD **Roman Rule** Last of the Gentile powers
Theme	God's sovereignty over kingdoms and His unfolding plan for the future			
Key Verses	2:20–22, 44; 4:34–37			
Christ in Daniel	The stone that will crush earth's kingdoms (2:34–35, 44); Son of Man (7:13–14); the coming Messiah who will be crucified (9:25–26)			

THE MINOR PROPHETS

The final twelve books of the Old Testament, Hosea to Malachi, make up what are called the Minor Prophets. The authors of these books began preaching in the middle of the ninth century BC and continued through the period of the kings on into the late fifth century BC, after the Jews returned to the Promised Land from their exile in Babylon. Like the major prophets, these men pronounced judgment and announced restoration, often exhorting the Israelite people to greater purity in their own lives, justice toward their neighbors, and humility before God.

HOSEA

Who Wrote the Book?

Hosea revealed little about his background, though his book of prophecy offers a few glimpses into his life. The prophet's name means "salvation," likely a reference to Hosea's position in Israel as a beacon of hope to those who would repent and turn to God because of his message.[1] Following the command of God, Hosea married Gomer, a bride God described as "a wife of harlotry" (Hosea 1:2) and a woman who bore Hosea three children, two sons and a daughter (1:4, 6, 9). God used the names of Hosea's children, along with his wife's unfaithfulness, to send specific messages to the people of Israel.

Where Are We?

In Hosea 1:1, the prophet identified the kings that ruled during his prophetic ministry. The first four—Uzziah, Jotham, Ahaz, and Hezekiah—reigned over the southern kingdom of Judah from 790 BC to 686 BC, while Jeroboam II ruled the northern kingdom of Israel from 782 BC to 753 BC. This indicates that Hosea lived in the middle to late eighth century BC (755–715 BC), making him a contemporary of the prophets Isaiah and Micah.

Hosea directed the early portion of his prophetic warnings to Jeroboam II, a descendant of the house of Jehu whose son, Zechariah, would soon come to ruin (Hosea 1:4; 2 Kings 15:8–12). Because this prophecy against the descendants of Jeroboam involved the birth of Hosea's children, we can conclude that he lived in the northern kingdom, where the names of his children would have had the greatest impact.

Why Is Hosea so Important?

More than any other prophet, Hosea linked his message closely with his personal life. By marrying a woman he knew would eventually betray his trust and by giving his children names that sent messages of judgment on Israel, Hosea's prophetic word flowed out of the life of his family. The cycle of repentance, redemption, and restoration evident in Hosea's prophecy—and even his marriage (Hosea 1:2; 3:1–3)—remains intimately connected to our lives. This sequence plays itself out in the lives of real people, reminding us that the Scriptures are far from a mere collection of abstract statements with no relation to real life. No, they work their way into our day-to-day existence, commenting on issues that impact all our actions and relationships.

What's the Big Idea?

Structured around five cycles of judgment and restoration, the book of Hosea makes clear its repetitious theme: though God will bring judgment on sin, He will always bring His people back to Himself. God's love for Israel, a nation of people more interested in themselves than in God's direction for their lives, shines through clearly against the darkness of their idolatry and injustice (Hosea 14:4).

Throughout the book, Hosea pictured the people turning away from the Lord and turning toward other gods (4:12–13; 8:5–6). This propensity for idolatry meant that the Israelites lived as if they were not God's people. And though God told them as much through the birth of Hosea's third child, Lo-ammi, He also reminded them that He would ultimately restore their relationship with Him, using the intimate and personal language of "sons" to describe His wayward people (1:9–10; 11:1).

How Do I Apply This?

Do you know the saving power of God, now offered to us through His Son, Jesus? If so, as a redeemed child of God, have you offered "redemption" or forgiveness to those in your life who were once under your judgment? Not only does the book of Hosea provide an example of God's love to a people who have left God behind, but it also shows us what forgiveness and restoration look like in a close relationship. The book of Hosea illustrates that no one is beyond the offer of our forgiveness because no one sits outside God's offer of forgiveness. Certainly, God brings judgment on those who turn from Him, but Hosea's powerful act of restoration within his own marriage set the bar high for those of us seeking godliness in our lives.

Hosea

	PERSONAL **The Agony of an Unfaithful Mate** Marriage Children Separation Reunion *CHAPTERS 1–3*		NATIONAL **The Tragedy of an Unfaithful People** Series of sermons declaring the sin of the people and the character of God Model of the message as Hosea remains true to his wife in spite of her infidelity *CHAPTERS 4–14*		
	Adulterous wife yet faithful husband		Adulterous nation yet faithful God		
	God: *"Go, take to yourself a wife of harlotry and have children of harlotry." (1:2)*	God: *"Go again, love a woman who is loved by her husband, yet an adulteress." (3:1)*	Nation is guilty God is holy	Nation needs judgment God is just	Nation has hope God is love
Theme	God's faithful love toward His unfaithful people				
Key Verses	2:19–20; 3:1; 11:1–12				
Christ in Hosea	Christ's being "called out" from hiding in Egypt as a child is pictured in Hosea's record of Israel's exodus from Egypt (11:1; see also Matthew 2:15). In Hosea's redemption of Gomer from the slave market, Christ is pictured as the loving, faithful Redeemer of sinful humanity.				

JOEL

Who Wrote the Book?

We know little of the prophet Joel beyond a few personal details contained in the book itself. He identified himself as the son of Pethuel, preached to the people of Judah, and expressed a great deal of interest in Jerusalem. Joel also made several comments on the priests and the temple, indicating a familiarity with the center of worship in Judah (Joel 1:13–14; 2:14, 17). Joel often drew upon natural imagery—the sun and the moon, the grass and the locusts—and in general seemed to understand the reality that truth must have an impact on us in the real world.

Where Are We?

Dating the writing of the book of Joel remains one of the most difficult tasks for Old Testament scholars because unlike most prophetic writers, Joel gave no explicit indication of his time period. In particular, Joel refrained from mentioning the current ruling kings. One of the most compelling arguments for dating the writing of the book of Joel explains this omission by suggesting the prophecy occurred in the aftermath of Judah's only ruling queen, Athaliah (d. 835 BC). Upon her death, she left only her young son, Joash, to rule. But because Joash was too young to rule, the priest Jehoida ruled in his place until he came of age. So if Joel prophesied during this caretaking period, it would make sense that he mentioned no official king. The book of Joel also makes ample mention of priests, temple rituals, and nations, such as Phoenicia, Philistia, Egypt, and Edom, that were prominent in the late ninth century BC. All of this points to a date of approximately 835 BC or soon after, making Joel one of the earliest writing prophets, as well as a contemporary of the prophet Elisha.

The book focuses its prophetic judgment on the southern kingdom of Judah with frequent references to Zion and the temple worship (Joel 1:13–14; 2:23, 32; 3:16, 21). Joel's familiarity with this area and the worship in the temple suggests that he lived in Judah, possibly even in the city of Jerusalem itself.

Why Is Joel so Important?

The book of Joel's importance to the canon of Scripture stems from its being the first to develop an oft-mentioned biblical idea: the day of the Lord. While Obadiah mentioned the terrifying event first (Obadiah 15), Joel's book gives some of the most striking and specific details in all of Scripture about the day of the Lord—days cloaked in darkness, armies that conquer like consuming fire, and the moon turning to blood. Rooted in such vibrant and physical imagery, this time of ultimate judgment, still future for us today (2 Thessalonians 2:2; 2 Peter 3:10), makes clear the seriousness of God's judgment on sin.

What's the Big Idea?

Using what was at that time the well-known locust plague in Judah, Joel capitalized on a recent tragedy to dispense the Lord's message of judgment and the hope of repentance. In referring to the terrible locust plague, Joel was able to speak into the lives of his listeners and imprint the message of judgment into their minds, like a brand sears the flesh of an animal.

One commentator notes that the day of the Lord, which is a reference not to a single day only but to a period of judgment and restoration, consists of three basic features:

- The judgment of God's people
- The judgment of foreign nations
- The purification and restoration of God's people through intense suffering[1]

We find each of these elements in the book of Joel, as it offers one of the most complete pictures in Scripture of this ultimately redemptive event (Joel 2:1–11; 2:28–32; 3:1–16).

How Do I Apply This?

Visions of the future, such as the kind we find in Joel or even in the pages of the more well-known book of Revelation, can often seem remote from our day-to-day existence. However, their vivid pictures of destruction should serve to awaken us from our spiritual stupor. Do you ever struggle with feeling complacent? A strong dose of apocalyptic imagery like we find in Joel might just do the trick of opening your eyes to the necessity of faithfully following after God every moment of your life.

JOEL

	The Plague of Locusts	The Call to Repentance	The Future of Judah	
	The past plague The future invasion Historic Day of the Lord Imminent Day of the Lord	"Return to Me" The character of God KEY: 2:13 The universal appeal	One of the greatest promises of hope in all the Old Testament	Concerning the Spirit of God Concerning the judgment of God Concerning the kingdom of God Ultimate Day of the Lord
	CHAPTERS 1:1–2:11	*CHAPTER 2:12–17*	*CHAPTER 2:18–27*	*CHAPTERS 2:28–3:21*
Emphasis	Desolation	Exhortation	Restoration	
Emotion	Mourning now → Rejoicing later			
Parallel Verse	"For His anger is but for a moment, His favor is for a lifetime; / Weeping may last for the night, / But a shout of joy comes in the morning" (Psalm 30:5).			
Theme	Repent, for the day of the Lord is near.			
Key Verses	2:12–14, 18, 25–27			
Christ in Joel	The coming of the Holy Spirit, who applies Christ's redemption, is predicted in 2:28. Jesus Christ is the One who judges nations but who also restores His people.			

AMOS

Who Wrote the Book?

The prophet Amos lived among a group of shepherds in Tekoa, a small town approximately ten miles south of Jerusalem. Amos made clear in his writings that he did not come from a family of prophets, nor did he even consider himself one. Rather, he was "a grower of sycamore figs" as well as a shepherd (Amos 7:14–15). Amos's connection to the simple life of the people made its way into the center of his prophecies, as he showed a heart for the oppressed and the voiceless in the world.

Where Are We?

Amos prophesied "two years before the earthquake" (Amos 1:1; see also Zechariah 14:5), just before the halfway point of the eighth century BC, during the reigns of Uzziah, king of Judah, and Jeroboam, king of Israel. Their reigns overlapped for fifteen years, from 767 BC to 753 BC.

Though he came from the southern kingdom of Judah, Amos delivered his prophecy against the northern kingdom of Israel and the surrounding nations, leading to some resistance from the prideful Israelites (Amos 7:12). Jeroboam's reign had been quite profitable for the northern kingdom, at least in a material sense. However, the moral decay that also occurred at that time counteracted any positives from the material growth.

Why Is Amos so Important?

Amos was fed up. While most of the prophets interspersed redemption and restoration in their prophecies against Israel and Judah, Amos devoted only the final five verses of his prophecy for such consolation.

Prior to that, God's word through Amos was directed against the privileged people of Israel, a people who had no love for their neighbor, who took advantage of others, and who only looked out for their own concerns.

More than almost any other book of Scripture, the book of Amos holds God's people accountable for their ill-treatment of others. It repeatedly points out the failure of the people to fully embrace God's idea of justice. They were selling off needy people for goods, taking advantage of the helpless, oppressing the poor, and the men were using women immorally (Amos 2:6–8; 3:10; 4:1; 5:11–12; 8:4–6). Drunk on their own economic success and intent on strengthening their financial position, the people had lost the concept of caring for one another; Amos rebuked them because he saw in that lifestyle evidence that Israel had forgotten God.

What's the Big Idea?

With the people of Israel in the north enjoying an almost unparalleled time of success, God decided to call a quiet shepherd and farmer to travel from his home in the less sinful south and carry a message of judgment to the Israelites. The people in the north used Amos's status as a foreigner as an excuse to ignore his message of judgment for a multiplicity of sins.

However, while their outer lives gleamed with the rays of success, their inner lives sank into a pit of moral decay. Rather than seeking out opportunities to do justice, love mercy, and walk humbly, they embraced their arrogance, idolatry, self-righteousness, and materialism. Amos communicated God's utter disdain for the hypocritical lives of His people (Amos 5:21–24). His prophecy concludes with only a brief glimpse of restoration, and even that is directed to Judah, rather than the northern kingdom of Israel (9:11–15).

How Do I Apply This?

Injustice permeates our world, yet as Christians we often turn a blind eye to the suffering of others for "more important" work like praying, preaching, and teaching. But the book of Amos reminds us that those works, while unquestionably central to a believer's life, ring hollow when we don't love and serve others in our own lives. Do you find yourself falling into that trap at times—prioritizing prayer over service?

The prophecy of Amos should simplify the choices in our lives. Instead of choosing between prayer and service, the book of Amos teaches us that both are essential. God has called Christians not only to be in relationship with Him but also to be in relationships with others. For those Christians whose tendency has been to focus more on the invisible God than on His visible creation, Amos pulls us back toward the center, where both the physical and the spiritual needs of people matter in God's scheme of justice.

AMOS

	Introduction	Oracles against the Nations	Sermons against Nation of Israel	Visions of Judgment	Promises of Hope
	A sheepherder's vision	Damascus / Gaza / Tyre / Edom / Ammon / Moab / Judah / Israel	Hear this word . . . sons of Israel (3:1) . . . you cows of Bashan (4:1) . . . house of Israel (5:1)	Locusts / Fire / Plumb line / Ripe fruit / The LORD by the altar	"In that day I will raise up the fallen booth of David. . . . I will also plant them on their land." (9:11,15)
	CHAPTER 1:1–2	*CHAPTERS 1:3–2:16*	*CHAPTERS 3–6*	*CHAPTERS 7:1–9:10*	*CHAPTER 9:11–15*
Theme	Israel's coming judgment for treating others with injustice.				
Key Verses	3:1–2; 4:12; 5:15, 24				
Christ in Amos	Jesus Christ, who has all authority to judge, is also the One who restores His people.				

OBADIAH

Who Wrote the Book?

In this, the shortest book of the Old Testament, it seems the prophet Obadiah considered each word a high-priced commodity. Apparently, he was unable to afford any words describing himself or his family in any way. Therefore, while twelve other men named Obadiah appear in Scripture, Old Testament scholars cannot identify with certainty any of them as the author of this book. Though the ultimate identity of this prophet is shrouded in mystery, Obadiah's emphasis on Jerusalem throughout this prophecy of judgment on the foreign nation of Edom, allows us at least to presume that Obadiah came from somewhere near the holy city in the southern kingdom of Judah.

Where Are We?

Dating the book of Obadiah accurately is nearly impossible due to the scant historical information contained in the book. While several options have been proposed by scholars, the best argument places Obadiah in the 840s BC, making him the earliest writing prophet, a few years prior to Joel, and a contemporary of Elisha. The biggest piece of evidence for this early date comes from Obadiah 1:10–14, which indicates an Edomite invasion of Jerusalem. While Edom was too weak a nation to ever invade Judah on its own, Edom no doubt participated with other nations when the winds of change blew in its favor.

In the 840s, when Edom rebelled against King Jehoram of Judah, the Philistines and the Arabians also invaded Jerusalem (2 Kings 8:20–22; 2 Chronicles 21:16–17). While 2 Chronicles does not indicate the Edomites' participation in the invasion, Obadiah 1:10–14 pictures the violent behavior that the Edomites carried out on their neighbors, waiting on nearby roads to cut down those fleeing from the invaders within Jerusalem. The Edomites could have easily heard of Jerusalem's invasion by foreign powers and entered themselves into the fray so that they too might benefit from plundering their neighbors in Jerusalem.

Why Is Obadiah so Important?

The majority of the book pronounces judgment on the foreign nation of Edom, making Obadiah one of only three prophets who pronounced judgment primarily on other nations (Nahum and Habakkuk are the others). While others of the prophetic books contain passages of judgment against Edom and other nations, Obadiah's singular focus points to a significant, albeit difficult, truth about humanity's relationship with God: when people remove themselves from or place themselves in opposition to God's people, they can expect judgment, rather than restoration, at the end of life.

What's the Big Idea?

Obadiah's name, meaning "worshipper of Yahweh," offers an interesting counterpoint to the message of judgment he pronounced on Edom, Judah's neighbor to the southeast.[1] As a worshipper of Yahweh, Obadiah placed himself in a position of humility before the Lord; he embraced his lowly place before the almighty God.

That God sent a man named "worshipper of Yahweh" to the people of Edom was no mistake. Edom had been found guilty of pride before the Lord (Obadiah 1:3). They had thought themselves greater than they actually were; great enough to mock, steal from, and even harm God's chosen people. But the "Lord God," a name Obadiah used to stress God's sovereign power over the nations, will not stand idly by and let His people suffer forever (1:1). Through Obadiah, God reminded Edom of their poor treatment of His people (1:12–14) and promised redemption, not to the Edomites but to the people of Judah (1:17–18). The nation of Edom, which eventually disappeared into history, remains one of the prime examples of the truth found in Proverbs 16:18: "Pride goes before destruction, / And a haughty spirit before stumbling."

How Do I Apply This?

Obadiah's prophecy focuses on the destructive power of pride. It reminds us of the consequences of living in a self-serving manner, of following through on our own feelings and desires without considering their impact on those around us. Do you struggle to set aside your own wants and desires for those of God and others? Though such pride has been part of the lives of fallen human beings since the tragedy of the fall in Eden, Obadiah offers us a stark reminder to place ourselves under God's authority, to subject our appetites to His purposes, and to find our hope in being His people when the restoration of all things comes.

OBADIAH

	Edom's Humiliation and Destruction *VERSES 1–9*	Edom's Cruelty and Crimes *VERSES 10–14*	Edom and the Day of the Lord *VERSES 15–21*
Portent	Prediction	Denunciation	Consummation
Event	What will happen	Why it will happen	How it will happen
Content	"The arrogance of your heart has deceived you. . . . I will bring you down." (1:3–4)	"Because of violence to your brother Jacob" (1:10)	"As you have done, it will be done to you." (1:15)
Theme	The coming judgment of Edom.		
Key Verse	1:10		
Christ in Obadiah	God's judgment of Edom and deliverance of Israel prefigure Christ's salvation and end-times judgment.		

JONAH

Who Wrote the Book?

The book of Jonah, written primarily in the third person, does not explicitly name the prophet as the author of his own account, but we have no reason to doubt either the inspiration or the historical veracity of the book. Identified in verse 1 as the son of Amittai, Jonah came from a town called Gath-hepher, near Nazareth in the area that later came to be known as Galilee (2 Kings 14:25). This makes Jonah one of the few prophets who hailed from the northern kingdom of Israel.

Where Are We?

During Jonah's years as a prophet, Israel stood tall among the nations, though in a political rather than a spiritual sense. The reign of Jeroboam II (793–753 BC), who was an evil king before the Lord, saw Israel's borders expand to their greatest extent since the time of Solomon. Increased prosperity resulted in a materialistic culture that thrived on injustice to the poor and oppressed, one of the key messages of Jonah's prophetic contemporary, Amos.

However, rather than direct Jonah to prophesy to his own people, God commissioned him to the Assyrian capital of Nineveh. At first unwilling to make the journey northeast to deliver God's message, Jonah turned and aimed for the farthest westward point known to him—Tarshish, located in modern-day Spain. After God eventually turned Jonah in the right direction, the prophet obediently prophesied to the people of Nineveh while Ashurdan III (772–754 BC) sat on the throne of Assyria. Though Assyria had been in a politically weakened state for some time, by the time of Jonah their cruelty to captives and other undesirables was well-known in Israel, creating an obvious need for Jonah's message of repentance.

Why Is Jonah so Important?

Jonah was one of only four writing prophets that Jesus mentioned by name during His earthly ministry (Isaiah, Daniel, and Zechariah were the others). But Jonah received more than a mere mention. Jesus actually identified Himself with the prophet's three-day sojourn in the belly of the great fish, noting it as a foreshadowing of His own death, when Jesus would spend three days "in the heart of the earth," before His resurrection (Matthew 12:39–41). Jesus's identification with the prophet at the lowest point of Jonah's life finds echoes in the book of Hebrews, where it teaches that Jesus "had to be made like His brethren in all things, so that He might become a merciful and faithful high priest" (Hebrews 2:17). The book of Jonah stands as an important link in the prophetic chain, giving readers a glimpse of Christ's death and resurrection hundreds of years before they actually occurred.

What's the Big Idea?

When the call of God came to him, Jonah could not see beyond his own selfish desire for God to punish the Assyrians. How could God want him to take a message of mercy to such people? Before Jonah could relay God's message, he had to be broken. He had to learn something about the mercy of the Lord. Through his flight to Tarshish, his shipwreck, and his time in the great fish, Jonah was convinced in a powerful way that all salvation comes from the Lord (Jonah 2:9). And because of God's supreme power, only God decides where to pour out His salvation and His mercy (4:11).

How Do I Apply This?

Do you ever find yourself fighting God—your desires pulling you one way, God's desires pulling you another? Jonah found himself in that very position, but his own desire won out over God's for a time. Or so he thought. As we often see in our own lives, God accomplished His purposes through Jonah even though it meant God doling out a heavy dose of humility on a prideful and unwilling heart.

While Jonah eventually departed and proclaimed God's message, the lesson of his story does not end there. Jonah prophesied to Nineveh but he wasn't happy about it (Jonah 4:1). Herein we find another touchstone for our lives: aligning our desires with God's is always a process. Just because we go through the motions of following God's will does not mean our hearts are aligned with His. God wanted Jonah's actions *and* his heart. He wants ours as well.

JONAH

	Running from God	Running to God	Running with God	Running against God
	First commission of Jonah	Prayer of Jonah	Second commission of Jonah	Prejudice of Jonah
	Results of disobedience	Communication with the Lord	Results of obedience	Lessons from the Lord
	CHAPTER 1	*CHAPTER 2*	*CHAPTER 3*	*CHAPTER 4*
Theme	God's infinite mercy for all people; our reluctance to share His mercy			
Key Verses	2:9; 4:11			
Christ in Jonah	Jonah's three days in the fish anticipates Christ's death and resurrection. The Ninevites' salvation represents the salvation available to all people in Christ.			

MICAH

Who Wrote the Book?

The prophet Micah identified himself by his hometown, called Moresheth Gath, which sat near the border of Philistia and Judah about twenty-five miles southwest of Jerusalem. Dwelling in a largely agricultural part of the country, Micah lived outside the governmental centers of power in his nation, leading to his strong concern for the lowly and less fortunate of society—the lame, the outcasts, and the afflicted (Micah 4:6). Therefore, Micah directed much of his prophecy toward the powerful leaders of Samaria and Jerusalem, the capital cities of Israel and Judah, respectively (1:1).

Where Are We?

As a contemporary of Isaiah and Hosea, Micah prophesied during the momentous years surrounding the tragic fall of Israel to the Assyrian Empire (722 BC), an event he also predicted (Micah 1:6). Micah stated in his introduction to the book that he prophesied during the reigns of Jotham, Ahaz, and Hezekiah in Judah, failing to mention the simultaneous string of dishonorable kings that closed out the northern kingdom of Israel.

During this period, while Israel was imploding from the effects of evil and unfaithful leadership, Judah seemed on a roller-coaster ride—ascending to the heights of its destiny in one generation, only to fall into the doldrums in another. In Judah at this time, good kings and evil kings alternated with each other, a pattern seen in the reigns of Jotham (good, 2 Kings 15:32–34); Ahaz (evil, 2 Kings 16:1–4); and Hezekiah (good, 2 Kings 18:1–7).

Why Is Micah so Important?

The book of Micah provides one of the most significant prophecies of Jesus Christ's birth in all the Old Testament, pointing some seven hundred years before Christ's birth to His birthplace of Bethlehem and to His eternal nature (Micah 5:2).

Surrounding Micah's prophecy of Jesus's birth is one of the most lucid pictures of the world's future under the reign of the Prince of Peace (5:5). This future kingdom, which scholars call the millennial kingdom, will be characterized by the presence of many nations living with one another in peace and security (4:3–4) and coming to Jerusalem to worship the reigning king, that is, Jesus Himself (4:2). Because these events have not yet occurred, we look forward to the millennial kingdom at some undetermined time in the future.

What's the Big Idea?

Much of Micah's book revolves around two significant predictions: one of judgment on Israel and Judah (Micah 1:1–3:12), the other of the restoration of God's people in the millennial kingdom (4:1–5:15). Judgment and restoration inspire fear and hope, two ideas wrapped up in the final sequence of Micah's prophecy, a courtroom scene in which God's people stand trial before their Creator for turning away from Him and from others (6:1–7:20). In this sequence, God reminds the people of His good works on their behalf, how He cared for them while they cared only for themselves. But rather than leave God's people with the fear and sting of judgment, the book of Micah concludes with the prophet's call on the Lord as his only source of salvation and mercy (7:7), pointing the people toward an everlasting hope in their everlasting God.

How Do I Apply This?

Much of Micah's indictment against Israel and Judah involves these nations' injustice toward the lowly—unjust business dealings, robbery, mistreatment of women and children, and a government that lived in luxury off the hard work of its nation's people.

Where does the injustice dwell in your own life? Who are the lowly in your life? Do you need a call toward repentance, like the people of Israel and Judah did?

Micah's impassioned plea for God's chosen people to repent will cut many of us to the quick. Most of us don't decide daily to cut people down or find ways to carry out injustice. Instead, we do it out of habit. Let's allow the words of Micah to break us out of our apathy about extending justice and kindness to others and press on toward a world that better resembles the harmonious millennial kingdom to come. Let's determine to live as God desires—"to do justice, to love kindness, and to walk humbly with our God" (Micah 6:8).

MICAH

	An Announcement of Judgment	A Contrast of Kingdoms	A Case against Sin and a Promise of Restoration
	Hear, O peoples . . . / Listen, O earth. (1:2)	*"Hear now, heads of Jacob / And rulers." (3:1)*	Hear now what the LORD is saying. (6:1)
	The capitals will be destroyed Reasons for judgment	Human corruption Divine restoration	God's indictment Authentic spirituality Judah's sins Messianic mercy
	CHAPTERS 1–2	*CHAPTERS 3–5*	*CHAPTERS 6–7*
Theme	Micah shows that a true relationship with God is inextricably linked to how we treat one another. He contrasts Judah's sinful kingdom with God's righteous and just messianic kingdom.		
Key Verse	6:8		
Christ in Micah	Jesus's birth in Bethlehem is predicted in 5:2; His righteous reign over all the earth is described in 2:12–13; 4:1–8; 5:4–5.		

NAHUM

Who Wrote the Book?

The only mention in Scripture of Nahum the Elkoshite occurs in the first verse of his own book. While scholars have proposed a number of theories about Nahum's hometown, Elkosh, the best option identifies it with a city in southern Judah that later came to be known as Elcesi, near where the prophet Micah lived. Nahum's prophecy against the city of Nineveh would have been significant for the people of Judah, who would have needed encouragement in the face of the terrifying power of the Assyrian Empire.

Where Are We?

The book of Nahum mentions the recent fall of No-amon, or Thebes, which occurred in 663 BC (Nahum 3:8), as well as the coming destruction of Nineveh, which happened in 612 BC (1:1; 3:11–15). But when, during this more than fifty-year period, did Nahum preach? The Assyrian Empire, which had its capital at Nineveh, was at its most powerful in the first half of this period, having a stranglehold on Judah during King Manesseh's reign (2 Chronicles 33:10–13). Also, while the book of Nahum mentions the destruction of Thebes, it does not mention its reconstruction, which took place in 654 BC. This leads us to date Nahum's prophecy between the years of 663 and 654 BC.

Nahum preached during the reign of King Manesseh, one of the most evil kings in Judah's long history, a man who needed the pain of his own experience to teach him the lessons of being a good king. Commentator J. Barton Payne suggests that Manasseh's great conversion took place late in his reign, around 648 BC, a mere half-dozen years before his death.[1] That means Nahum preached during the darkest period in Judah's history to that point, a time filled with idolatry of all kinds in a nation that had completely turned its back on God. The Lord's willingness to send Nahum, whose name means "comfort," into such a hopeless situation evidences His unrelenting and overwhelming grace.[2]

Why Is Nahum so Important?

Nahum's singular focus on the impending judgment of Nineveh offers a continuation of the story that began in Jonah. Sometime around 760 BC, God sent Jonah to Nineveh to preach repentance and hope to the Assyrian people, a message they heard and adopted—at least for a time. One hundred years later, during the time of Nahum, the Assyrians had returned to their bullish ways, conquering the northern kingdom of Israel and lording their power over Judah in the south (2 Kings 17:1–6; 18:13–19:37). Jonah failed to realize what Nahum reminded the people of Judah: God's justice is always right and always sure. Should He choose to grant mercy for a time, that good gift will not compromise the Lord's ultimate sense of justice for all in the end.

What's the Big Idea?

After allowing approximately two hundred years of powerful Assyrian kings and rulers, God announced through Nahum His plans to judge the city of Nineveh. While the book as a whole clearly shows God's concern over sin, His willingness to punish those guilty of wickedness, and His power to carry out His desire for judgment, it also contains rays of hope shining through the darkness. Most significant, the people of Judah would have immediately taken hope in the idea that Nineveh, their primary oppressor for generations, would soon come under judgment from God. Also, a small but faithful remnant in an increasingly idolatrous Judah would have been comforted by declarations of God's slowness to anger (Nahum 1:3), His goodness and strength (1:7), and His restorative power (2:2).

How Do I Apply This?

No doubt we all have felt overwhelmed by the darkness both within ourselves and in our world. Nahum lived in a dark time, a time in which the faithful few must have wondered how long they would have to resist cultural and spiritual compromise.

Have you ever found your will to do what's right weakening as you became discouraged with what you saw in your life and in the world around you? The prophet Nahum reminds us of God's active hand, working even in the darkest of times to bring justice and hope throughout the world.

NAHUM

	The Character and Power of God	**The Judgment of God**
	His majestic attributes and abilities in contrast to humanity's schemes	Predicted and described Justified and defended Inevitable and inescapable
	CHAPTER 1	*CHAPTERS 2–3*
Content	Theological	Prophetical
Emphasis	The majestic character of our sovereign God qualifies Him to be the Judge over all.	Nineveh's willful and heartless decline justifies the judgment of almighty God.
Theme	The impending doom of Ninevah, capital of Assyria	
Key Verses	1:3; 3:1	
Christ in Nahum	Christ will judge the nations, freeing His people once and for all from their enemies.	

HABAKKUK

Who Wrote the Book?

We know little of Habakkuk beyond the two mentions of his name in this book of prophecy. Both times, he identified himself as "Habakkuk the prophet" (Habakkuk 1:1; 3:1), a term that seems to indicate Habakkuk was a professional prophet. This could mean that Habakkuk was trained in the Law of Moses in a prophetic school, an institution for educating prophets that cropped up after the days of Samuel (1 Samuel 19:20; 2 Kings 4:38). Habakkuk also could have been a priest involved with the worship of God at the temple. This assumption is based on the book's final, psalm-like statement: "For the choir director, on my stringed instruments" (Habakkuk 3:19).

Where Are We?

Determining the date of the book of Habakkuk is quite a bit easier than dating most books. He spoke often of an imminent Babylonian invasion (Habakkuk 1:6; 2:1; 3:16), an event that occurred on a smaller scale in 605 BC before the total destruction of Judah's capital city, Jerusalem, in 586 BC. The way Habakkuk described Judah indicates a low time in its history. If the dating is to remain close to the Babylonian invasion, Habakkuk likely prophesied in the first five years of Jehoiakim's reign (609–598 BC) to a king who led his people into evil.

Habakkuk's prophecy was directed to a world that, through the eyes of God's people, must have seemed on the edge of disaster. Even when the northern kingdom had been destroyed in 722 BC, God's people remained in Judah. However, with another powerful foreign army on the rampage, faithful people like Habakkuk were wondering what God was doing. Hadn't He given the land to His people? Would He now take it away? Habakkuk's prayer of faith for the remainder of God's people in the face of such destruction still stands today as a remarkable witness of true faith and undying hope.

Why Is Habakkuk so Important?

Habakkuk provides us one of the most remarkable sections in all of Scripture, as it contains an extended dialogue between Habakkuk and God (Habakkuk 1–2). The prophet initiated this conversation based on his distress about God's "inaction" in the world. He wanted to see God do something more, particularly in the area of justice for evildoers. The book of Habakkuk pictures a frustrated prophet, much like Jonah, though Habakkuk channeled his frustration into prayers and eventually praise to God, rather than trying to run from the Lord as Jonah did.

What's the Big Idea?

As the prophet Habakkuk stood in Jerusalem and pondered the state of his nation, Judah, he must have been dumbfounded. So much evil thrived, completely in the open, but God remained strangely silent. Where was He? How long would He allow this mess to continue? Not long, according to the Lord (Habakkuk 2:2–3). Another nation, the Babylonians, would come and execute justice on the Lord's behalf. The wicked in Judah, those who thought they would get away with their evil deeds forever, were soon to be punished.

The book of Habakkuk offers us a picture of a prideful people being humbled, while the righteous live by faith in God (2:4). It reminds us that while God may seem silent and uninvolved in our world, He always has a plan to deal with evil and always works out justice . . . eventually. The example of the prophet Habakkuk encourages believers to wait on the Lord, expecting that He will indeed work out all things for our good (Romans 8:28).

How Do I Apply This?

Habakkuk asked God the kind of question that so many of us have pondered, "Why do you force me to look at evil, / stare trouble in the face day after day?" (Habakkuk 1:3 MSG). We have all seen the evidence of evil in our lives. We've all been touched by it. And we bear scars at various stages of healing. Surrounded by evil as if we are trapped in a dark prison cell of our own making, we are often downtrodden by our poor choices and our fallen world. However, the book of Habakkuk reminds us that no place is too dark and no wall too thick for God's grace to penetrate in a powerful and life-affirming way.

HABAKKUK

	Habakkuk's Dialogue with God			Habakkuk's Praise to God
	The Burden	***The Watch***	***The Vision***	
	Wrestling with: God's silence Judah's sinfulness God's character Questions: How long? Why? Who?	Waiting for an answer	Record the vision! Wait for it! Woe to the Babylonians!	Lord, I've heard . . . I stand in awe . . . I wait . . . I praise . . . I rejoice
	CHAPTER 1	*CHAPTER 2:1*	*CHAPTER 2:2–20*	*CHAPTER 3*
Confession	"Lord . . . You confuse me."	"Lord . . . I wait for You."		"Lord . . . I praise You."
Perspective	Horizontal	Vertical		
Direction	Looking around and worrying	Looking up and listening		Looking ahead and believing
Theme	Habakkuk's wrestling with God over His unfathomable ways and the prophet's resulting faith			
Key Verses	2:4; 3:17–19			
Christ in Habakkuk	Those who have been made righteous in Christ must "live by [their] faith" (2:4). When Christ comes again, "the earth will be filled / With the knowledge of the glory of the LORD, / As the waters cover the sea" (2:14).			

ZEPHANIAH

Who Wrote the Book?

In Zephaniah 1:1, the author introduces himself as "Zephaniah son of Cushi, son of Gedaliah, son of Amariah, son of Hezekiah." Among the prophets, this is a unique introduction with its long list of fathers back to Zephaniah's great-great grandfather, Hezekiah. So why stop with Hezekiah? Most likely, the prophet wanted to highlight his royal lineage as a descendant of one of Judah's good kings. The reference to "this place" in Zephaniah 1:4 indicates that he prophesied in Jerusalem, while his many references to temple worship display a strong familiarity with Israel's religious culture. All these factors paint the picture of a man who was at the center of Judah's political and religious world, a man whose close proximity to those in power would have given his shocking message an even greater impact.

Where Are We?

The book tells us that Zephaniah prophesied during the reign of Josiah, the king of Judah from 640 to 609 BC (Zephaniah 1:1). We can begin to pinpoint exactly when Zephaniah prophesied by accounting for a few details in the text. First, in 2:13 the prophet predicted the fall of Nineveh, an event which occurred in 612 BC. Further, Zephaniah made frequent quotations from the Law (for example, compare 1:13 to Deuteronomy 28.30, 39), a document that remained lost in Judah for much of Josiah's reign. Therefore, Zephaniah more than likely prophesied in the latter part of Josiah's rule, after the king discovered the scrolls of the Law in 622 BC (2 Chronicles 34:3–7).

Zephaniah

	Judgment and Doom "I will completely remove all things from the face of the earth," declares the LORD. (1:2)				Joy and Deliverance
INTRODUCTION (1:1)	DIVINE JUDGMENT ON JUDAH	INVITATION	SURE DOOM OF NATIONS	SURE DOOM OF JERUSALEM	KINGDOM PROMISES TO REMNANT
	CHAPTER 1:2–18	*CHAPTER 2:1–3*	*CHAPTER 2:4–15*	*CHAPTER 3:1–8*	*CHAPTER 3:9–20*
Scope	Judah		Nations		Remnant
Subject	Sin	Hope	Desolation		Restoration
Key Words	"The day of the LORD"	"Seek"	"Woe"		The LORD is with you
Theme	Judgment and doom are certain unless there is repentance before God. Only then can there be hope and restoration.				
Key Verses	1:14; 2:3				
Christ in Zephaniah	Jesus Christ hides us from God's wrath, and is the One who will someday rule the earth as King of Israel (Zephaniah 3:15–17; see Colossians 3:3–4).				

HAGGAI

Who Wrote the Book?

The prophet Haggai recorded his four messages to the Jewish people of Jerusalem in 520 BC, eighteen years after their return from exile in Babylon (538 BC). Haggai 2:3 seems to indicate that the prophet had seen Jerusalem before the destruction of the temple and the exile in 586 BC, meaning he was more than seventy years old by the time he delivered his prophecies. From these facts, the picture of Haggai begins to come into focus. He was an older man looking back on the glories of his nation, a prophet imbued with a passionate desire to see his people rise up from the ashes of exile and reclaim their rightful place as God's light to the nations.

Where Are We?

Haggai's prophecy came at a time when the people of Judah were extremely vulnerable. They had been humbled by their exile to Babylon, hopeful in their return to their Promised Land, and then so discouraged by opposition in their rebuilding of the temple that they had quit (Ezra 4:24). Now, sixteen years later, with Haggai blaming their lack of food, clothing, and shelter on their failure to rebuild the temple, the Jews were receptive to his message of rebuilding the Lord's house.

Unlike most of the other prophets, Haggai explicitly dated his prophecies, down to the day. He gave four separate messages, the first on August 29, 520 BC (Haggai 1:1); the second on October 17, 520 BC (2:1); and the final two on December 18, 520 BC (2:10, 20). These messages encouraged the people of Judah to finish building the temple and to have hope in God for the promise of blessings in the future.

HAGGAI

	"First day of the sixth month" (1:1) — "Twenty-fourth day of the sixth month" (1:15)		"Twenty-first [day] of the seventh month" (2:1) — "Twenty-fourth [day] of the ninth month" (2:10)
	First Message: **Rebuild God's temple** Rebuke Reflection Divine discipline Repentant response "I am with you" *CHAPTER 1*	Almost a month of silence	**Second, Third and Fourth Messages:** **Encouragement and Hope** "Take courage!" "I will bless you!" "I have chosen you!" *CHAPTER 2*
Time	Twenty-three days		Over two months
Emphasis	Practical, negative, confronting		Spiritual, positive, comforting
Scope	Present condition of Jerusalem temple		Future glory of God's house
Theme	We must put God first in order to experience His blessings.		
Key Verses	1:4–5; 2:7–9		
Christ in Haggai	Christ's presence in this temple, which was further expanded and adorned by Herod, is "the latter glory . . . greater than the former" (2:9). Jesus is "our peace" (Ephesians 2:14). His death on the cross has made us at peace with God now, and His future rule in His glorious Kingdom will establish worldwide peace (Haggai 2:9). The righteous leader Zerubbabel is also a type of Christ and part of Jesus's genealogy.		

ZECHARIAH

Who Wrote the Book?

Grandson of the priest Iddo, Zechariah prophesied to the people of Judah after they returned from their seventy years of exile in Babylon (Zechariah 1:1; Nehemiah 12:1, 4, 16). Zechariah's grandfather returned from Babylon, his young grandson in tow, with the first group of Israelites allowed back, in 538 BC under the decree of Cyrus, king of Persia. Because of his family lineage, Zechariah was a priest in addition to a prophet. He, therefore, would have had an intimate familiarity with the worship practices of the Jews, even if he had never served in a completed temple. As a "young man" at the time of his first prophecies (Zechariah 2:4), his life more than likely extended into the reign of Xerxes I (485–465 BC), the king best known in the Bible for making Esther the queen of Persia (Esther 1:1).[1]

Where Are We?

Zechariah, a young man, especially when compared to his contemporary Haggai, came alongside the older prophet to deliver messages from the Lord to the Jewish remnant recently returned from Babylon. While Haggai's overall message had more of a cautionary tone to it (pointing out the Jews' sin and self-focus), Zechariah emphasized a tone of encouragement to the struggling Israelites trying to rebuild their temple.

Zechariah's dated visions and messages in chapters 1–8 all take place in the same general time period as Haggai's, beginning in October–November 520 BC with a call for the people of Judah to repent (Zechariah 1:1). He then received eight visions on the restless night of February 15, 519 BC (1:7), followed by four messages that

ZECHARIAH

	Call to Repentance	Encouragement and Motivation	Questions	Encouragement and Hope
		Visions Horses and riders Horns and craftsmen Surveyor and measuring line Joshua (the priest) and Satan Lampstand and seven lights Flying scroll and warning Woman and a basket Chariots and judgment	Fasting Failure Future of Zion	**Predictions** **First "Oracle":** Rejection of Messiah Preservation of Israel Deception of false prophets **Second "Oracle":** Israel's final victory Messiah's final victory
	CHAPTER 1:1–6	*CHAPTERS 1:7–6:15*	*CHAPTERS 7–8*	*CHAPTERS 9–14*
Time	Written during the building of the temple			Written after completion of the temple
Purpose	To motivate those working on the temple to continue in spite of their own crop failures and financial distress. Rather than rebuking or condemning, Zechariah inspired the people to work.			To give the workers hope that there was a better day, a far more glorious day yet to come. Vivid scenes of Messiah are included. He is revealed as coming, rejected, returning, and conquering.
Theme	Build the temple; build your future			
Key Verses	4:6; 8:3; 9:9–10			
Christ in Zechariah	Zechariah is second only to Isaiah in its number of messianic passages. Among Zechariah's explicit references to Christ are the angel of the Lord (3:1–2); the righteous Branch (3:8; 6:12–13); the King-Priest (6:13); the cornerstone, tent peg, and bow of battle (10:4); the good shepherd who is sold for thirty pieces of silver (11:4–13); the pierced One (12:10); and the coming Judge and righteous King (14).			

MALACHI

Who Wrote the Book?

The final book of the Old Testament, Malachi received its name from its author (Malachi 1:1). In Hebrew, the name comes from a word meaning "messenger," which points to Malachi's role as a prophet of the Lord, delivering God's message to God's people.[1] Malachi offered no other identifying information about himself, leaving out markers typical of other prophets such as his father's name or the current leader of Israel.

However, based on the content of the book, it becomes clear that Malachi delivered his message of judgment to a Judean audience familiar with worshipping at the temple in Jerusalem (2:11). The people of Judah had turned away from the true worship of the Lord, leaving themselves under judgment and in need of salvation.

Where Are We?

Malachi certainly wrote to the people of Judah (Malachi 1:1; 2:11), but the historical setting becomes clearer in Malachi 1:8. Here the prophet used the Persian word for governor, indicating a time period between 538–333 BC, when the Persian Empire ruled the Promised Land. Malachi also wrote about the corruption of the temple sacrifices, meaning that he likely delivered his message many years after the Israelites rebuilt the temple in 515 BC. The prophet's concerns mirror those of Nehemiah's, suggesting that Malachi prophesied to the people while Nehemiah left the city for several years, beginning in 432 BC (Nehemiah 13:6).

MALACHI

	Love	Rebuke		Hope
		Against the Priests	Against the People	
	Unconditional Almighty Sovereign	Irreverence Disobedience Cynicism Hypocrisy Offense	Intermarriage with pagans Indifference Robbing God / no tithes Blasphemy	Fire Healing "Elijah" Family
	CHAPTER 1:1–5	*CHAPTERS 1:6–2:9*	*CHAPTERS 2:10–3:15*	*CHAPTERS 3:16–4:6*
Content	Theological	Historical		Prophetical
Direction	Looking up	Looking in		Looking ahead
Theme	God cites the priest and the people with failure to keep His covenant but offers the hope of the Messiah, the messenger of the covenant who will bring justice and salvation.			
Key Verse	3:1			
Christ in Malachi	Malachi anticipates the first and second advents of Christ, who will fulfill God's covenant with the Jews (3:1), judge sinners (3:2–5), and bring healing to those who fear the Lord (4:2).			

Appendixes

MAP OF THE PENTATEUCH, PART ONE

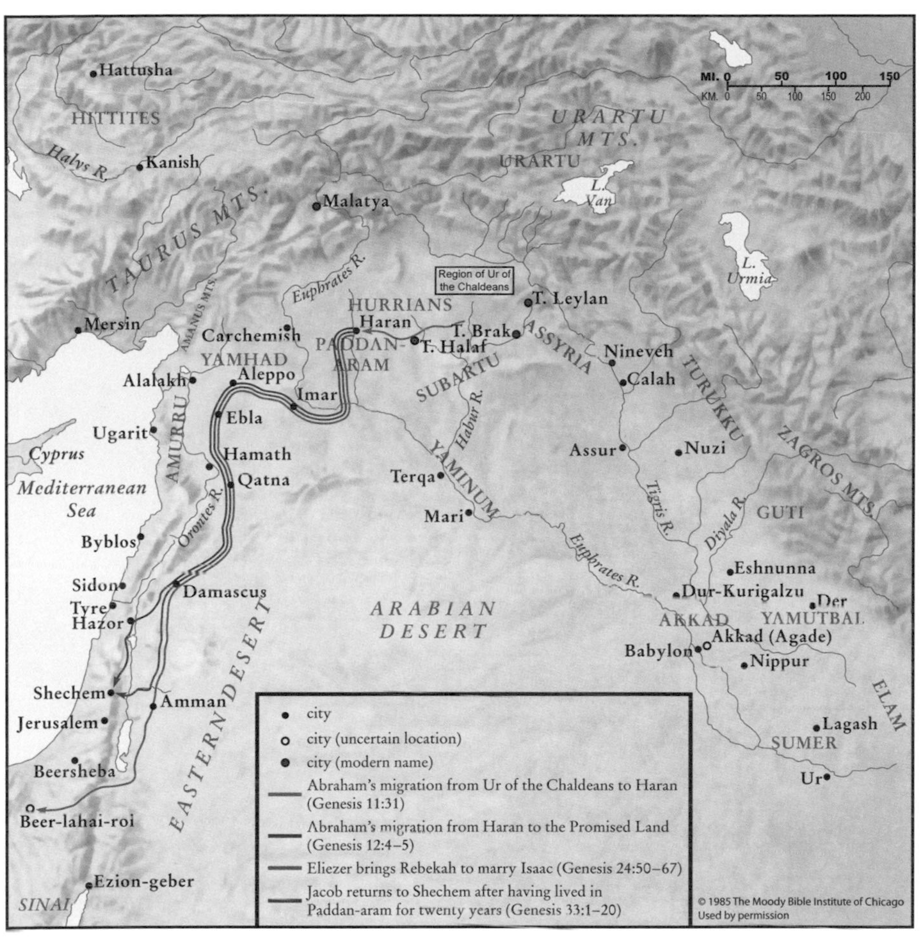

MAP OF THE PENTATEUCH, PART TWO

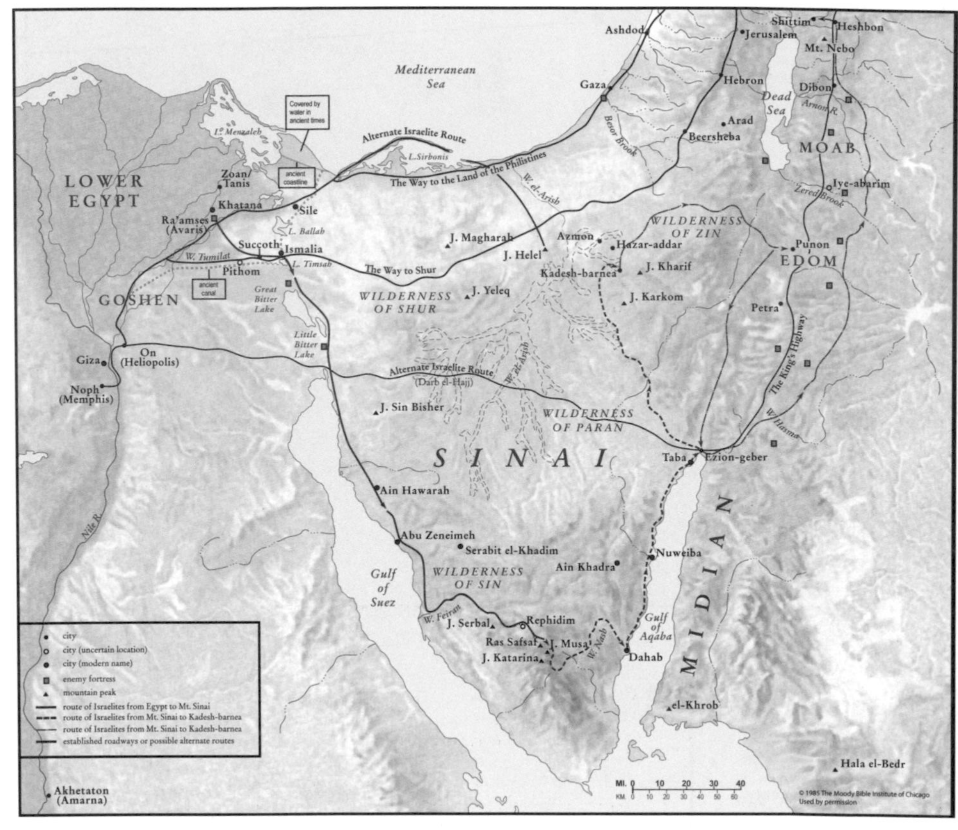

MAP OF THE UNITED KINGDOM

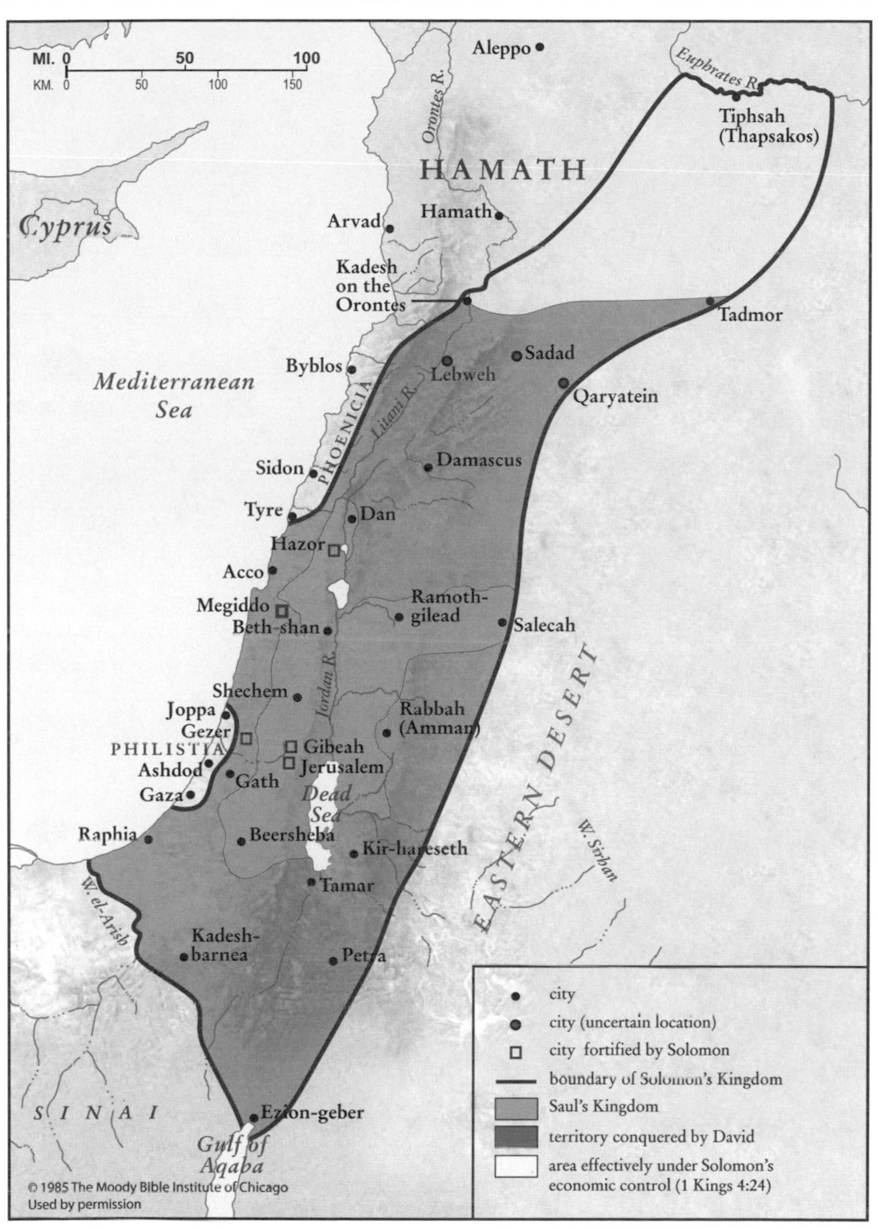

MAP OF THE DIVIDED KINGDOM

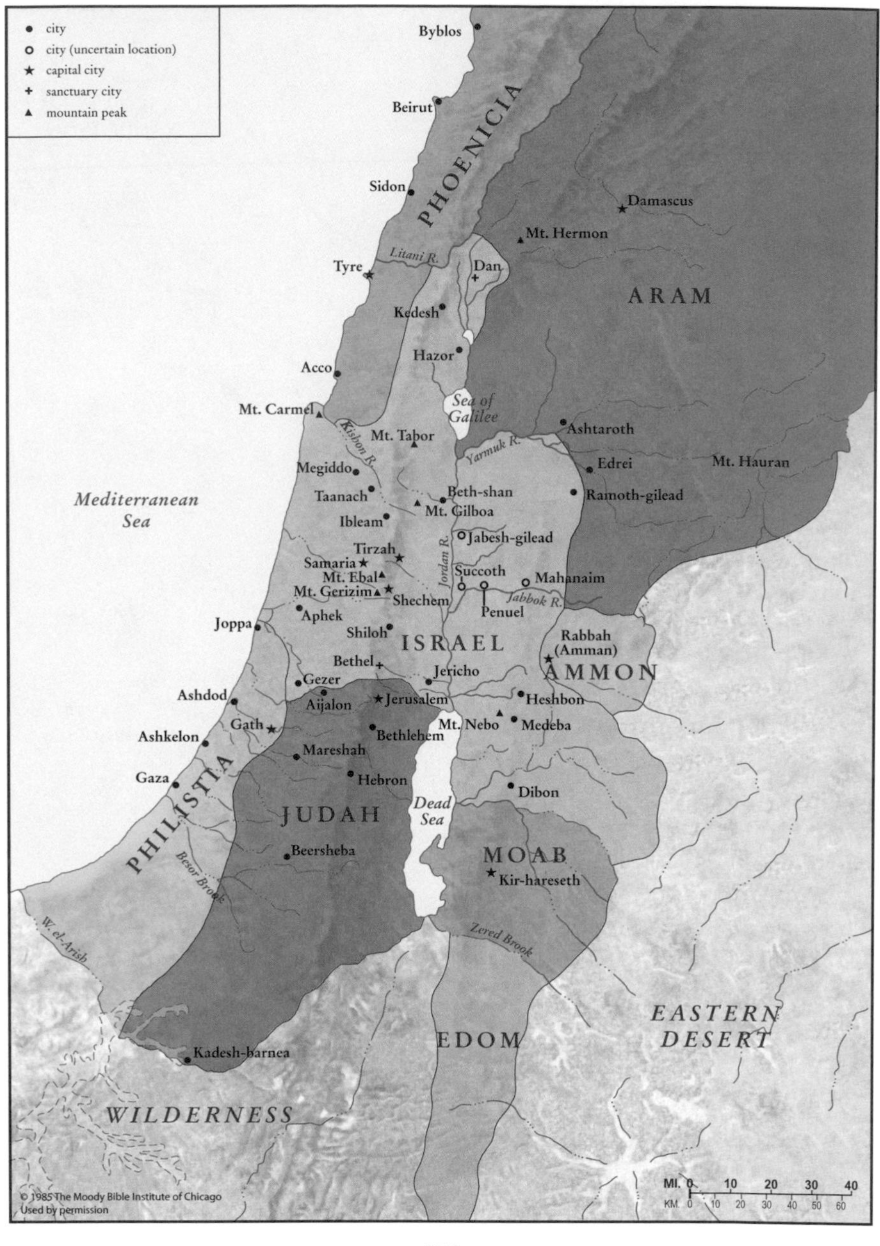

MAP OF THE EXILE AND RETURNS

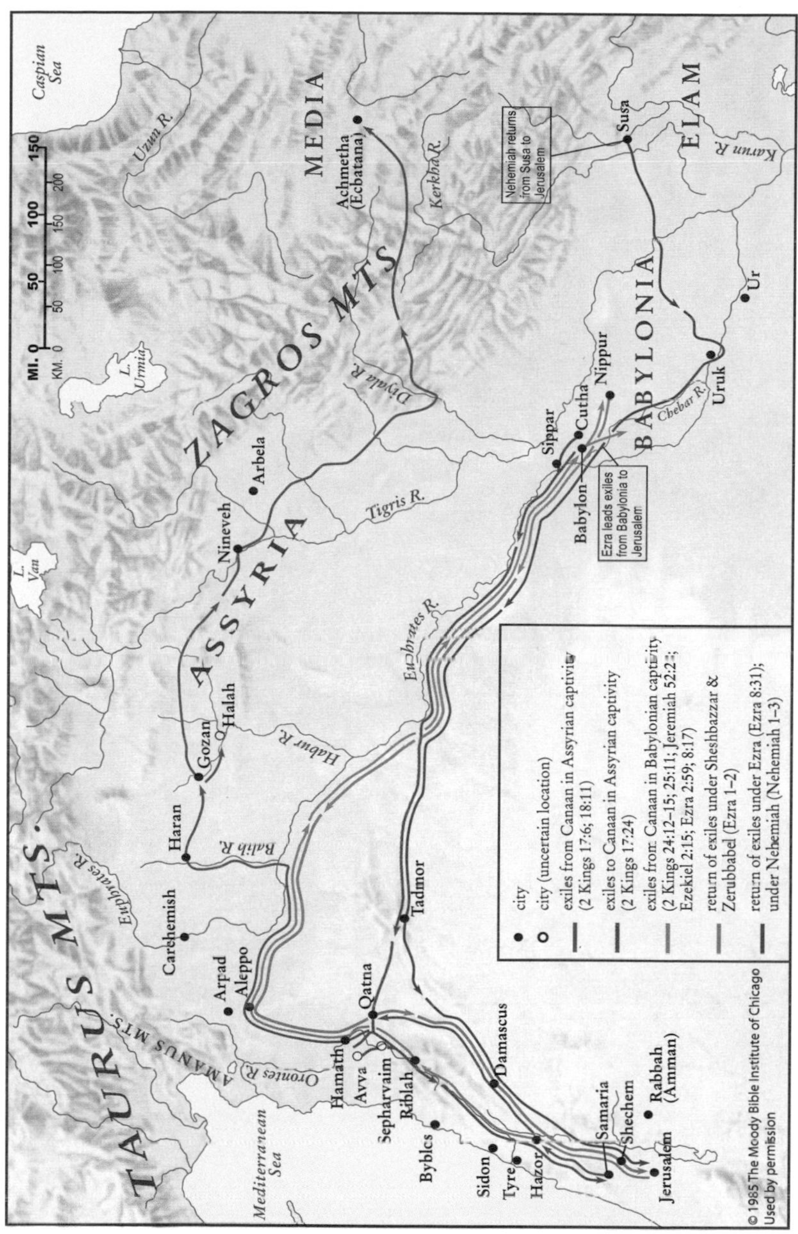

Appendix B

Timeline of Old Testament Books and Events

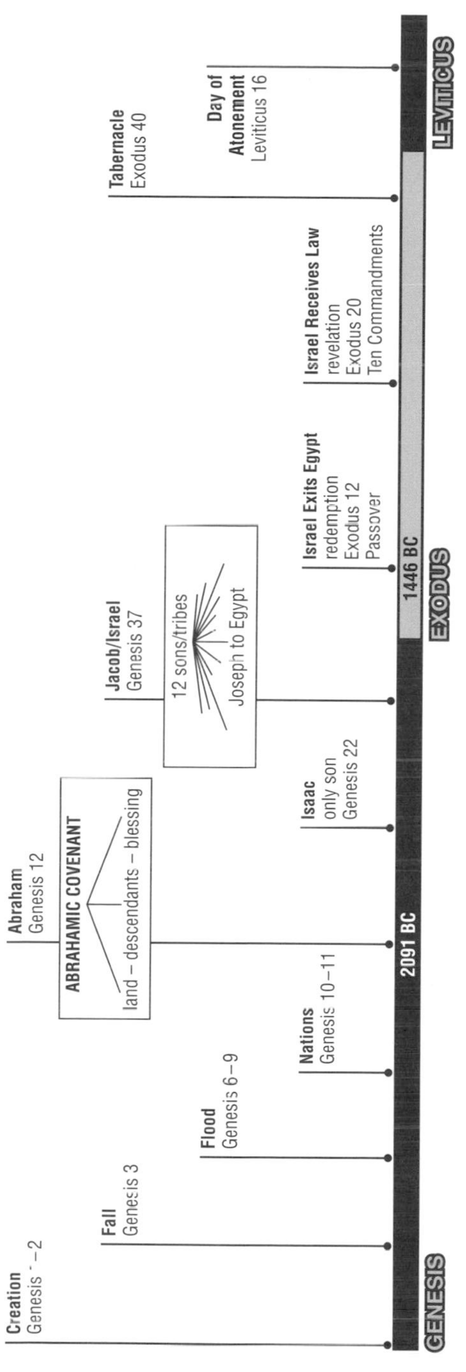

Legend: PENTATEUCH • **HISTORICAL BOOKS** • *Wisdom Books* • ***Prophetical Books***

TIMELINE OF OLD TESTAMENT BOOKS AND EVENTS, CONT.

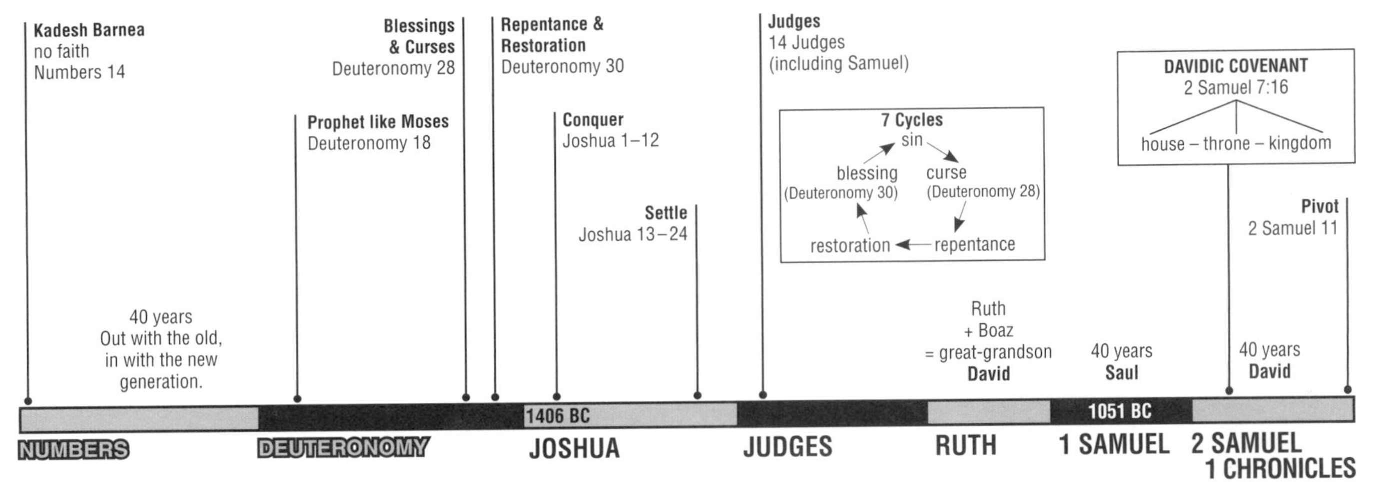

Legend: PENTATEUCH • HISTORICAL BOOKS • *Wisdom Books* • ***Prophetical Books***

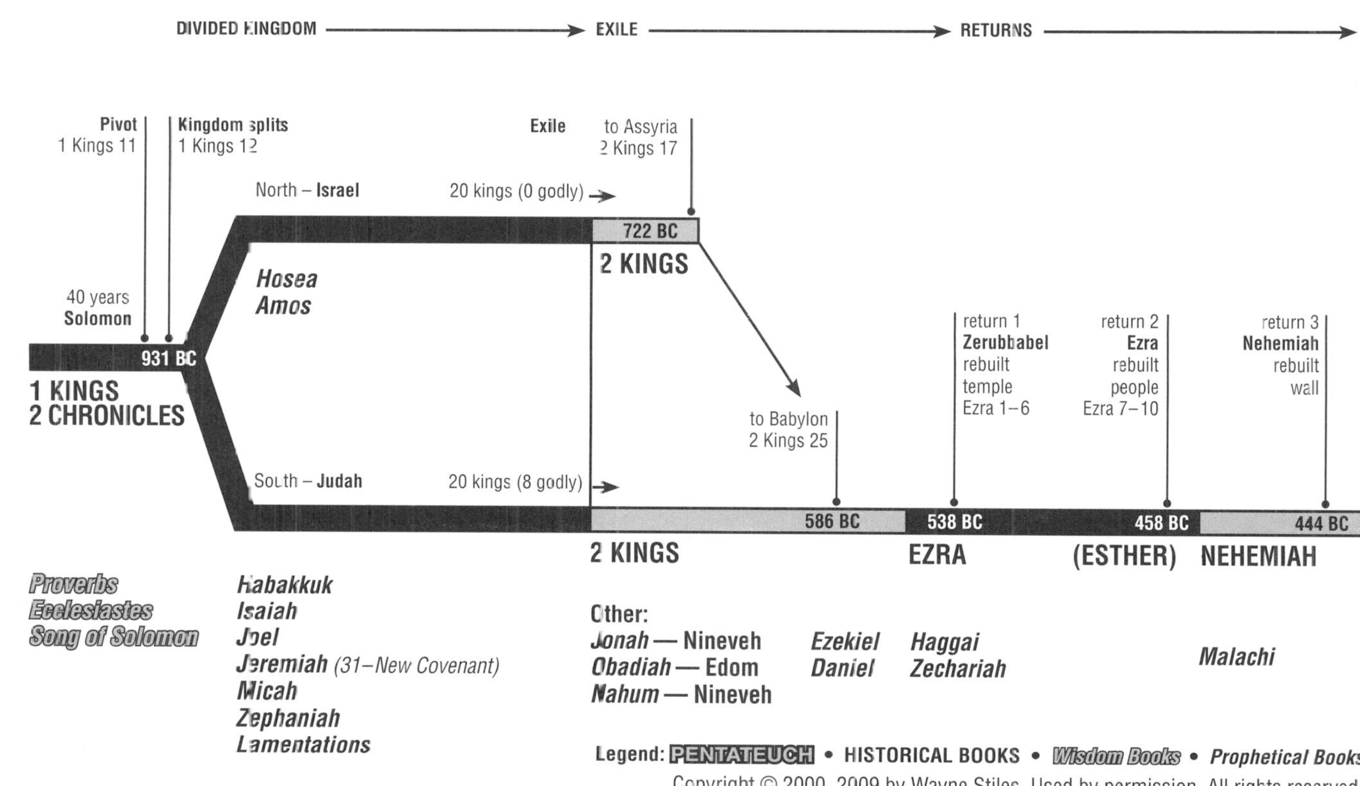
TIMELINE OF OLD TESTAMENT BOOKS AND EVENTS, CONT.
DIVIDED KINGDOM
EXILE
RETURNS
Pivot
1 Kings 11
Kingdom splits
1 Kings 12
Exile
to Assyria
2 Kings 17
North – Israel
20 kings (0 godly)
40 years
Solomon
931 BC
722 BC
2 KINGS
Hosea
Amos
1 KINGS
2 CHRONICLES
to Babylon
2 Kings 25
return 1
Zerubbabel
rebuilt
temple
Ezra 1–6
return 2
Ezra
rebuilt
people
Ezra 7–10
return 3
Nehemiah
rebuilt
wall
South – Judah
20 kings (8 godly)
586 BC
538 BC
458 BC
444 BC
2 KINGS
EZRA
(ESTHER)
NEHEMIAH
Proverbs
Ecclesiastes
Song of Solomon
Habakkuk
Isaiah
Joel
Jeremiah (31–New Covenant)
Micah
Zephaniah
Lamentations
Other:
Jonah — Nineveh
Obadiah — Edom
Nahum — Nineveh
Ezekiel
Daniel
Haggai
Zechariah
Malachi
Legend: PENTATEUCH • HISTORICAL BOOKS • Wisdom Books • Prophetical Books
Copyright © 2000, 2009 by Wayne Stiles. Used by permission. All rights reserved.

Appendix C

CHRONOLOGY OF THE OLD TESTAMENT PROPHETS

Prophet	Approximate Date BC	Kings of Israel and Judah	Dominant Powers	Passages for Historical Context
Obadiah	848–841	Israel: Jehoram Judah: Joram	Philistia Assyria	2 Kings 3:1–27; 8:16–9:26 2 Chronicles 21:4–20
Joel	835	Israel: Joash Judah: Jehu	Assyria	2 Kings 9–12 2 Chronicles 22:10–24:27
Jonah	772–754	Israel: Jeroboam II Judah: Amaziah and Uzziah	Assyria	2 Kings 14:1–15:7 2 Chronicles 26
Amos	767–753	Israel: Jeroboam II Judah: Uzziah	Assyria	2 Kings 14:23–15:7 2 Chronicles 26
Hosea	755–715	Israel: Jeroboam II, Zechariah, Shallum, Menahem, Pekahiah, Pekah, Hoshea Judah: Uzziah, Jotham, Ahaz, Hezekiah	Assyria	2 Kings 14:23–17:6; 18–20 2 Chronicles 26–32
Isaiah	739–681	Israel: Pekah, Hoshea Judah: Uzziah, Jotham, Ahaz, Hezekiah, Manasseh	Assyria	2 Kings 15:1–7; 16:27–17:6; 18:1–21:17 2 Chronicles 26:1–33:20

Prophet	Approximate Date BC	Kings of Israel and Judah	Dominant Powers	Passages for Historical Context
Micah	735–710	Israel: Pekah, Hoshea Judah: Jotham, Ahaz, Hezekiah	Assyria	2 Kings 15:27–17:6; 18–20 2 Chronicles 27–32
Nahum	663–654	Judah: Manasseh	Assyria	2 Kings 21:1–18 2 Chronicles 33:1–20
Jeremiah	627–582	Judah: Josiah, Jehoahaz, Jehoiakim, Jehoiachin, Zedekiah	Assyria Babylon	2 Kings 22–25 2 Chronicles 34–36
Zephaniah	622–612	Judah: Josiah	Assyria	2 Kings 22:1–23:30 2 Chronicles 34–35
Habakkuk	609–604	Judah: Jehoiakim	Babylon	2 Kings 23:36–24:7 2 Chronicles 36:5–8
Daniel	605–536	Judah: Jehoiakim, Jehoiachin, Zedekiah	Babylon	2 Kings 23:36–25:30 2 Chronicles 36:5–23
Ezekiel	593–571	Judah: Zedekiah	Babylon	2 Kings 24:18–25:30 2 Chronicles 36:11–23
Haggai	520	Judah: Zerubbabel (governor)	Medo-Persia	Ezra 1–6
Zechariah	520–480	Judah: Zerubbabel (governor)	Medo-Persia	Ezra 1–6
Malachi	432	Judah: Nehemiah (governor)	Medo-Persia	Nehemiah 1–13

Appendix D

THE BIBLE THAT EARLY CHRISTIANS USED

Translations of the Old Testament

Only a couple of decades after the death and resurrection of Jesus, small communities of Christians found themselves scattered throughout an often-hostile Roman Empire. They received occasional visits from luminaries such as Paul or Peter, but they had no apostle consistently on the scene to teach them. Because most of the earliest Christians were Jewish, they at least had their knowledge of the Hebrew Scriptures to guide them until a letter came from Paul or a gospel by John was circulated. But what did their Bible look like, how did it come to those early Christians, and most significant for today, how has it come to us?

Hebrew Bible

The Old Testament was originally written in Hebrew within the Israelite community over the course of about a thousand years between the 1400s BC (Moses) and the 400s BC (Malachi). Copied and recopied throughout that period, the first manuscripts of the Old Testament now in our possession came soon after Malachi, during the third through first centuries BC. These early manuscripts record only the consonants of the words—no vowels—which was the standard practice of writing Hebrew in the ancient period. Eventually, the Jewish community established an authoritative version of the Hebrew text by AD 135, and within a few hundred years, a group called the Masoretes added vowels and accents to the text for easier reading. Due to the work of the Masoretes on this project, we now recognize their efforts by calling the Hebrew Bible with vowels the Masoretic Text.[1]

Septuagint

Looking back to a time in the middle of the third century BC, the ancient Letter to Aristeas tells of seventy-two Jewish scholars who came together in Alexandria, Egypt, to translate the books of the Hebrew Bible into Greek.[2] The Greek language had been gaining ground throughout the world since the time of Alexander the Great (336–323 BC). So when the rulers in Alexandria after Alexander decided to collect the great works throughout the known world, the Hebrew Bible was high on the list.

This Greek translation of the Old Testament came to be known as the *Septuagint* (meaning "seventy"), a Greek word referring to the (approximately) seventy men who worked on the initial translation (often designated in Roman numerals as LXX). Their work began in Alexandria with the translation of the Pentateuch (Genesis through Deuteronomy), and as the decades passed, other scholars began to translate the rest of the Old Testament. By the end of the second century BC, the translation of the entire Old Testament was complete.[3]

Initially, the Septuagint was quite popular in the Jewish community, with significant authors such as Philo and Josephus using it almost exclusively. The Greek translation also allowed the Jewish community outside of Judea to flourish, because increasingly, Jews living outside the Holy Land knew Greek better than Hebrew.

High regard for the Septuagint extended to the apostles of Jesus, who more often than not cited the Old Testament from the Septuagint, rather than from the Hebrew Bible. Paul in particular made ample use of the Septuagint. Because Paul's primary ministry was to Greek-speaking Gentiles, it makes sense that he quoted the translation of the Bible most understandable to his hearers.

The prominence of the Septuagint also played a role in the expansion of the Christian church throughout the Greek-speaking Roman Empire. During the earliest decades after Christ's death and resurrection, the Old Testament was the only Bible the Christians possessed. That it was available in Greek made the Word of God that much more accessible to people in all corners of the world throughout the early centuries of the church. The popularity of the Greek Old Testament in the Christian community was no doubt the significant factor in the Jews' eventual rejection of the Septuagint in favor of the original Hebrew or other Greek versions that were produced.

Vulgate

As Latin became more and more common throughout the western part of the Roman Empire in the second and third centuries AD, scholars composed a Latin translation of the Septuagint, called the Old Latin Bible. However, due to the poor quality of the translation, Pope Damasus I commissioned a Christian named Jerome in AD 382 to create a new Latin translation. After several smaller revisions, Jerome became convinced of the need to translate directly from the Hebrew text. So from AD 390 to 405, Jerome worked tirelessly on his translation, which came to be known as the Vulgate. While the Vulgate eventually became the dominant Bible in the Roman Catholic Church, it took approximately three hundred years before it gained equal footing with the earlier Old Latin translation.[4]

Conclusion

Between the late fourteenth and early sixteenth centuries, early Roman Catholic radicals, such as John Wycliffe and John Huss, and later Reformers, such as Martin Luther and John Calvin, advocated for Bible translations in the languages of the people to whom they ministered. When first written, the Old Testament was in Hebrew. When Christianity came on the scene, it was translated into Greek. As Latin developed, the Bible appeared in that language. All three were the language of the people at the time, but as years passed, these languages were forgotten by the common people and new translations were needed in new languages. We should consider ourselves grateful to those who've gone before us, who so tirelessly and meticulously translated the Old Testament into languages the populace could read and understand, for we have that same privilege today.

Appendix E

THE APOCRYPHA

Why Are Some Books "Missing"?

The *canon*, or "rule," of Scripture denotes the authoritative list of books that belong to the Old and New Testaments. What qualifies a book to belong to this sacred body of religious writings? The book must be ancient, informative and helpful, valued and read by God's people, and—primarily—have God's authority. We know the Scriptures are authoritative because they are inspired (2 Timothy 3:16). In other words, the Bible comes from God, given to us by God through His followers who faithfully recorded His words of revelation to us (2 Peter 1:20–21).

So why then do some English translations of the Bible differ in the number of Old Testament books they include? The answer takes us back to the ancient Jewish scholars and the fathers of the Christian church.

A Question of Canon

The thirty-nine Old Testament books we have introduced in this handbook reflect the canon of the Hebrew Scriptures that Jesus and religious leaders of His day accepted as authoritative. These books were originally written in Hebrew or Aramaic. But also present in the ancient Jewish world were additional well-known writings written in Greek. These works gained attention by claiming to be authored by an individual known from the Bible, such as Adam or Enoch, by their strong Jewish cultural and religious content, and frequently, by their apocalyptic or visionary nature. Many of these pseudepigraphal books, or "false inscriptions," were written in the four hundred "silent" years between the end of the Old Testament prophets and the coming of John the Baptist.

A core group of pseudepigraphal works from this era came to be called Apocrypha, meaning "hidden [or] spurious."[1] When the Hebrew Bible was translated into Greek (a translation known as the Septuagint and often designated with the Roman numerals LXX), some of these apocryphal books were appended to the collection of biblical books in the Septuagint. Different copies of the Septuagint included different apocrypha. The collection of accepted works varied by region and culture. Yet none of the apocryphal books attained the full status of inspired, canonical works in the earliest centuries of the church. References to apocryphal books cannot be found in the New Testament, whose authors were aware of their existence. Even the book of Jude's possible quotation from the book of Enoch (Jude 1:14–15) does not mean that Jude regarded it as Scripture. Paul also included quotations from non-scriptural sources in his letters and sermons (Acts 17:28; 1 Corinthians 15:33; Titus 1:12).

Christians reading the Septuagint were certainly familiar with the apocryphal books. As one scholar wrote, "The Apocrypha were known in the church from the start, but the further back one goes, the more rarely are they treated as inspired."[2] The Septuagint continued to be the primary resource for Christians, the vast majority of whom spoke Greek. Early Christian bishops such as Melito of Sardis (AD 170) and Athanasius of Alexandria (AD 367) who wrote out lists of biblical books either left out the Apocrypha altogether or specifically labeled the apocryphal books as non-canonical. As centuries passed and church leadership became fixed in Rome, Christians developed Latin translations from the Septuagint.

Jerome

When the church father Jerome (AD 347–420) began a new translation of the Bible into Latin, he used the Hebrew Bible instead of the Septuagint to translate the Old Testament. While Jerome initially rejected the Apocrypha completely, he eventually collected the apocryphal books into a separate section of his Latin translation, allowing that they were useful for edification but not for establishing doctrine. Jerome's Latin translation, known as the Vulgate, ultimately became the primary translation for the Catholic church, with the Apocrypha regularly included in new copies of the Bible and referenced alongside Scripture.

The Reformation

In the early sixteenth century, Martin Luther reaffirmed Jerome's position and included the Apocrypha as a separate section in his German translation of the Bible. For Luther, the apocryphal books were helpful for the Christian life but not inspired. Roman Catholic leaders, at the Council of Trent in 1546, reacted to the Protestant Reformation by affirming the inspiration of the *entire* Vulgate—including the Apocrypha.[3] Roman Catholic Bibles now refer to the Apocrypha as "deuterocanonical," meaning "second canon," because they were written and collected after the "first," or Hebrew, canon.

Today

The Catholic and Eastern Orthodox traditions continue to affirm the inspiration of the Apocrypha. The following works are included in translations by the Roman Catholic church today:

- Tobit
- Judith
- Additions to Esther
- Wisdom of Solomon
- Ecclesiasticus, or the Wisdom of Jesus ben Sirach
- Baruch
- Additions to the book of Daniel (the Prayer of Azariah and the Song of the Three Young Men, Susanna, Bel and the Dragon)
- 1 Maccabees
- 2 Maccabees

Among Protestants, the Anglican Church continues to include the apocryphal books in a separate section, affirming their usefulness for edification but not for doctrine. However, most modern Protestant translators now eliminate the Apocrypha entirely from editions of the Bible, including in the Old Testament only those thirty-nine books found in the Hebrew canon affirmed by Jesus, the New Testament authors, and the earliest Christian lists of biblical books.

HOW TO BEGIN A RELATIONSHIP WITH GOD

Since sin and its consequences entered the world with the fall of Adam and Eve in Genesis 3, human beings have yearned for a better life . . . usually without looking in the right place for it. Because God loves His creation, throughout history He has used men and women who love Him to proclaim the truth in both word and deed so that we *can* have a better life—an eternal life with God. The lives of the individuals we study in the Old Testament are a testimony to the powerful ways that God can work in our lives to bring us back to Him. If you're interested in beginning a relationship with God, the Bible marks the path with four essential truths. Let's look at each marker in detail.

Our Spiritual Condition: Totally Depraved

The first truth is rather personal. One look in the mirror of Scripture, and our human condition becomes painfully clear:

> "There is none righteous, not even one;
> There is none who understands,
> There is none who seeks for God;
> All have turned aside, together they have become
> useless;
> There is none who does good,
> There is not even one." (Romans 3:10–12)

We are all sinners through and through—totally depraved. Now, that doesn't mean we've committed every atrocity known to humankind. We're not as *bad* as we can be, just as *bad off* as we can be. Sin colors all our thoughts, motives, words, and actions.

You still don't believe it? Look around. Everything around us bears the smudge marks of our sinful nature. In spite of our best efforts to create a perfect world, crime statistics continue to soar, divorce rates keep climbing, and families keep crumbling.

Something has gone terribly wrong in our society and in ourselves—something deadly. Contrary to how the world would repackage it, "me-first" living doesn't equal rugged individuality and freedom; it equals death. As Paul said in his letter to the Romans, "The wages of sin is death" (Romans 6:23)—our spiritual and physical death that comes from God's righteous judgment of our sin, along with all of the emotional and practical effects of this separation that we experience on a daily basis. This brings us to the second marker: God's character.

God's Character: Infinitely Holy

How can God judge each of us for a sinful state we were born into? Our total depravity is only half the answer. The other half is God's infinite holiness.

The fact that we know things are not as they should be points us to a standard of goodness beyond ourselves. Our sense of injustice in life on this side of eternity implies a perfect standard of justice beyond our reality. That standard and source is God Himself. And God's standard of holiness contrasts starkly with our sinful condition.

Scripture says that "God is Light, and in Him there is no darkness at all" (1 John 1:5). God is absolutely holy—which creates a problem for us. If He is so pure, how can we who are so impure relate to Him?

Perhaps we could try being better people, try to tilt the balance in favor of our good deeds, or seek out methods for self-improvement. Throughout history, people have attempted to live up to God's standard by keeping the Ten Commandments or living by their own code of ethics. Unfortunately, no one can come close to satisfying the demands of God's law. Romans 3:20 says, "By the works of the Law no flesh will be justified in His sight; for through the Law comes the knowledge of sin."

Our Need: A Substitute

So here we are, sinners by nature and sinners by choice, trying to pull ourselves up by our own bootstraps to attain a relationship with our holy Creator. But every time we try, we fall flat on our faces. We can't live a good enough life to make up for our sin, because God's standard isn't "good enough"—it's *perfection*. And we can't make amends for the offense our sin has created without dying for it.

Who can get us out of this mess?

If someone could live perfectly, honoring God's law, and would bear sin's death penalty for us—in our place—then we would be saved from our predicament. But is there such a person? Thankfully, yes!

Meet your substitute—*Jesus Christ*. He is the One who took death's place for you!

> [God] made [Jesus Christ] who knew no sin to be sin on our behalf, so that we might become the righteousness of God in Him. (2 Corinthians 5:21)

God's Provision: A Savior

God rescued us by sending His Son, Jesus, to die on the cross for our sins (1 John 4:9–10). Jesus was fully human and fully divine (John 1:1, 18), a truth that ensures His understanding of our weaknesses, His power to forgive, and His ability to bridge the gap between God and us (Romans 5:6–11). In short, we are "justified as a gift by His grace through the redemption which is in Christ Jesus" (3:24). Two words in this verse bear further explanation: *justified* and *redemption*.

Justification is God's act of mercy, in which He declares righteous the believing sinners while we are still in our sinning state. Justification doesn't mean that God *makes* us righteous, so that we never sin again, rather that He *declares* us righteous—much like a judge pardons a guilty criminal. Because Jesus took our sin upon Himself and suffered our judgment on the cross, God forgives our debt and proclaims us PARDONED.

Redemption is Christ's act of paying the complete price to release us from sin's bondage. God sent His Son to bear His wrath for all of our sins—past, present, and future (Romans 3:24–26; 2 Corinthians 5:21). In humble obedience, Christ willingly endured the shame of the cross for our sake (Mark 10:45; Romans 5:6–8; Philippians 2:8). Christ's death satisfied God's righteous demands. He no longer holds our sins against us, because His own Son paid the penalty for them. We are freed from the slave market of sin, never to be enslaved again!

Placing Your Faith in Christ

These four truths describe how God has provided a way to Himself through Jesus Christ. Because the price has been paid in full by God, we must respond to His free gift of eternal life in total faith and confidence in Him to save us. We must step forward into the relationship with God that He has prepared for us—not by doing good works or by being a good person but by coming to Him just as we are and accepting His justification and redemption by faith.

> For by grace you have been saved through faith; and that not of yourselves, it is the gift of God; not as a result of works, so that no one may boast. (Ephesians 2:8–9)

We accept God's gift of salvation simply by placing our faith in Christ alone for the forgiveness of our sins. Would you like to enter a relationship with your Creator by trusting in Christ as your Savior? If so, here's a simple prayer you can use to express your faith:

> *Dear God,*
>
> *I know that my sin has put a barrier between You and me. Thank You for sending Your Son, Jesus, to die in my place. I trust in Jesus alone to forgive my sins, and I accept His gift of eternal life. I ask Jesus to be my personal Savior and the Lord of my life. Thank You. In Jesus's name, amen.*

If you've prayed this prayer or one like it and you wish to find out more about knowing God and His plan for you in the Bible, contact us at Insight for Living. Our contact information is on the following pages.

WE ARE HERE FOR YOU

If you desire to find out more about knowing God and His plan for you in the Bible, contact us. Insight for Living provides staff pastors who are available for free written correspondence or phone consultation. These seminary-trained and seasoned counselors have years of experience and are well-qualified guides for your spiritual journey.

Please feel welcome to contact your regional Pastoral Ministries by using the information below:

United States
Insight for Living
Pastoral Ministries
Post Office Box 269000
Plano, Texas 75026-9000
USA
972-473-5097, Monday through Friday,
8:00 a.m.–5:00 p.m. Central time
www.insight.org/contactapastor

Canada
Insight for Living Canada
Pastoral Ministries
Post Office Box 2510
Vancouver, BC V6B 3W7
CANADA
1-800-663-7639
info@insightforliving.ca

Australia, New Zealand, and South Pacific
Insight for Living Australia
Pastoral Care
Post Office Box 443
Boronia, VIC 3155
AUSTRALIA
1 300 467 444

United Kingdom and Europe
Insight for Living United Kingdom
Pastoral Care
Post Office Box 348
Leatherhead
KT22 2DS
UNITED KINGDOM
0800 915 9364
+44 (0) 1372 370 055
pastoralcare@insightforliving.org.uk

ENDNOTES

Genesis

1. Walter Bauer and others, eds., *A Greek-English Lexicon of the New Testament and Other Early Christian Literature*, 2d rev. ed. (Chicago: University of Chicago Press, 1979), 154.

Leviticus

1. Raymond B. Dillard and Tremper Longman, III, *An Introduction to the Old Testament* (Grand Rapids: Zondervan, 1994), 73.

2. F. Duane Lindsey, "Leviticus," in *The Bible Knowledge Commentary: Old Testament*, ed. John F. Walvoord and Roy B. Zuck (Wheaton, Ill.: Victor Books, 1985), 163.

3. Lindsey, "Leviticus," 166.

Numbers

1. Eugene H. Merrill, "Numbers," *The Bible Knowledge Commentary: Old Testament*, ed. John F. Walvoord and Roy B. Zuck (Wheaton, Ill.: Victor Books, 1985), 215.

Deuteronomy

1. Merrill F. Unger, *Unger's Commentary on the Old Testament* (Chattanooga, Tenn.: AMG, 2002), 233.

Joshua

1. Donald K. Campbell, "Joshua," in *The Bible Knowledge Commentary: Old Testament*, ed. John F. Walvoord and Roy B. Zuck (Wheaton, Ill.: Victor Books, 1985), 325.

2. Norman L. Geisler, *A Popular Survey of the Old Testament* (Peabody, Mass.: Prince Press, 2007), 93–94.

Ruth

1. Carolyn Custis James, *The Gospel of Ruth: Loving God Enough to Break the Rules* (Grand Rapids: Zondervan, 2008), 28.

First Samuel

1. Normal L. Geisler, *A Popular Survey of the Old Testament* (Peabody, Mass.: Prince Press, 2007), 107.

Second Samuel

1. Lawrence O. Richards, *The Teacher's Commentary* (Wheaton, Ill.: Victor Books, 1987), electronic ed., accessed through Libronix Digital Library System.

First Kings

1. See Thomas L. Constable, "1 Kings," in *The Bible Knowledge Commentary: Old Testament*, ed. John F. Walvoord and Roy B. Zuck (Wheaton, Ill.: Victor Books, 1985), 483.

2. Constable, "1 Kings," 484.

3. Merrill F. Unger, *Unger's Commentary on the Old Testament* (Chattanooga, Tenn.: AMG, 2002), 447.

First Chronicles

1. Eugene H. Merrill, "1 Chronicles," in *The Bible Knowledge Commentary: Old Testament*, ed. John F. Walvoord and Roy B. Zuck (Wheaton, Ill.: Victor Books, 1985), 589.

2. Larry Richards, *The Bible Reader's Companion* (Wheaton, Ill.: Victor Books, 1991), electronic ed., accessed through Libronix Digital Library System.

3. Richards, *The Bible Reader's Companion*.

Second Chronicles

1. Larry Richards, *The Bible Reader's Companion* (Wheaton, Ill.: Victor Books, 1991), electronic ed., accessed through Libronix Digital Library System.

2. Richards, *The Bible Reader's Companion.*

3. Richards, *The Bible Reader's Companion.*

Nehemiah

1. Norman L. Geisler, *A Popular Survey of the Old Testament* (Peabody, Mass.: Prince Press, 2007), 165.

Job

1. Roy B. Zuck, "Job," in *The Bible Knowledge Commentary: Old Testament*, ed. John F. Walvoord and Roy B. Zuck (Wheaton, Ill.: Victor Books, 1985), 718.

Psalms

1. Thomas L. Constable, "Notes on Psalms," 2009 ed., Sonic Light, 1, http://www.soniclight.com/constable/notes/pdf/psalms.pdf, accessed June 1, 2009.

Proverbs

1. Allen P. Ross, "Proverbs," in *The Expositor's Bible Commentary: Old Testament*, abridged ed., ed. Kenneth L. Barker and John R. Kohlenberger III (Grand Rapids: Zondervan, 1994), 938.

Song of Solomon

1. Dennis F. Kinlaw, "Song of Songs," in *The Expositor's Bible Commentary: Old Testament*, abridged ed., ed. Kenneth L. Barker and John R. Kohlenberger III (Grand Rapids: Zondervan, 1994), 1027.

2. Tom Gledhill, *The Message of the Song of Songs: The Lyrics of Love* (Downers Grove, Ill.: InterVarsity, 1994), 35.

Isaiah

1. Justin Martyr, *Dialogue with Trypho*, 120.5, trans. Thomas B. Falls, ed. Michael Slusser (Washington DC: Catholic University of America Press, 2003), 181.

2. Francis Brown, S. R. Driver, and Charles A. Briggs, *The Brown-Driver-Briggs Hebrew and English Lexicon* (Peabody, Mass.: Hendrickson, 2006), 447.

Lamentations

1. Charles H. Dyer, "Lamentations," in *The Bible Knowledge Commentary: Old Testament*, ed. John F. Walvoord and Roy B. Zuck (Wheaton, Ill.: Victor Books, 1985), 1207.

Hosea

1. Francis Brown, S. R. Driver, and Charles A. Briggs, *The Brown-Driver-Briggs Hebrew and English Lexicon* (Peabody, Mass.: Hendrickson, 2006), 448.

Joel

1. Robert B. Chisholm, Jr., "Joel," in *The Bible Knowledge Commentary: Old Testament*, ed. John F. Walvoord and Roy B. Zuck (Wheaton, Ill.: Victor Books, 1985), 1412.

Obadiah

1. Walter L. Baker, "Obadiah," in *The Bible Knowledge Commentary: Old Testament*, ed. John F. Walvoord and Roy B. Zuck (Wheaton, Ill.: Victor Books, 1985), 1453.

Zechariah

1. Following the Hebrew text, many translations of Esther call the king of Persia Ahasuerus, the Hebrew name for Xerxes.

2. F. Duane Lindsey, "Zechariah," in *The Bible Knowledge Commentary: Old Testament*, ed. John F. Walvoord and Roy B. Zuck (Wheaton, Ill.: Victor Books, 1985), 1545.

Malachi

1. Francis Brown, S. R. Driver, and Charles A. Briggs, *The Brown-Driver-Briggs Hebrew and English Lexicon* (Peabody, Mass.: Hendrickson, 2006), 521.

Appendix D
The Bible That Early Christians Used

1. Ellis R. Brotzman, *Old Testament Textual Criticism: A Practical Introduction* (Grand Rapids: Baker Books, 1998), 43–44, 52–53.

2. Alfred Rahlfs, "History of the Septuagint Text," in *Septuaginta* (Stuttgart: Deutsche Bibelgesellschaft, 1979), LVI.

3. Rahlfs, "History of the Septuagint Text," LVI.

4. Brotzman, *Old Testament Textual Criticism*, 82.

Appendix E
The Apocrypha

1. M. G. Easton, *Easton's Bible Dictionary* (Oak Harbor, Wash.: Logos Research Systems, 1996), electronic ed., accessed through Libronix Digital Library System.

2. D. R. W. Wood and I. Howard Marshall, *New Bible Dictionary*, 3d ed. (Downers Grove: Ill.: InterVarsity, 1996), electronic ed., accessed through Libronix Digital Library System.

3. Eastern Orthodox churches also deemed the Apocrypha "genuine Scripture" at the councils of Jassy (1642) and Jerusalem (1672).

RESOURCES FOR PROBING FURTHER

To further your study of the Old Testament, we recommend the following resources. Of course, we cannot always endorse everything a writer or ministry says, so we encourage you to approach these and all other non-biblical resources with wisdom and discernment.

Barker, Kenneth L., and John R. Kohlenberger III, eds. *The Expositor's Bible Commentary: Old Testament*. Abridged ed. Grand Rapids: Zondervan, 1994.

Beitzel, Barry J. *The Moody Atlas of Bible Lands*. Chicago: Moody Press, 1985.

Chisholm, Robert B., Jr. *Interpreting the Minor Prophets*. Grand Rapids: Zondervan, 1990.

Dyer, Charles, and Gene Merrill. *The Old Testament Explorer: Discovering the Essence, Background, and Meaning of Every Book in the Old Testament*. Nashville: Thomas Nelson, 2001.

Jensen, Irving. *Jensen's Survey of the Old Testament*. Chicago: Moody Publishers, 1978.

Merrill, Eugene H. *Kingdom of Priests: A History of Old Testament Israel*. 2nd ed. Grand Rapids: Baker Academic, 2008.

Radmacher, Earl D., Ronald B. Allen, and H. W. House, eds. *Nelson's New Illustrated Bible Commentary: Spreading The Light Of God's Word Into Your Life*. Nashville: Thomas Nelson, 1999.

Tenney, Merril C., ed. *Zondervan's Pictorial Bible Dictionary*. Grand Rapids: Zondervan, 1967.

Walton, John H. *Chronological and Background Charts of the Old Testament*. Rev. ed. Grand Rapids: Zondervan, 1994.

Walvoord, John F., and Roy B. Zuck, eds. *The Bible Knowledge Commentary: Old Testament*. Wheaton, Ill.: Victor Books, 1985.

Wiersbe, Warren W. *The Wiersbe Bible Commentary: Old Testament*. Colorado Springs: David C. Cook, 2007.

Yancey, Philip. *The Bible Jesus Read*. Grand Rapids: Zondervan, 1999.

ORDERING INFORMATION

If you would like to order additional copies of *Insight's Old Testament Handbook: A Practical Look at Each Book* or order other Insight for Living resources, please contact the office that serves you.

United States

Insight for Living
Post Office Box 269000
Plano, Texas 75026-9000
USA
1-800-772-8888 (Monday through Friday,
7:00 a.m.–7:00 p.m. Central time)
www.insight.org
www.insightworld.org

Canada

Insight for Living Canada
Post Office Box 2510
Vancouver, BC V6B 3W7
CANADA
1-800-663-7639
www.insightforliving.ca

Australia, New Zealand, and South Pacific

Insight for Living Australia
Post Office Box 443
Boronia, VIC 3155
AUSTRALIA
1 300 467 444
www.insight.asn.au

United Kingdom and Europe

Insight for Living United Kingdom
Post Office Box 348
Leatherhead
KT22 2DS
UNITED KINGDOM
0800 915 9364
www.insightforliving.org.uk

Other International Locations

International constituents may contact the U.S. office through our Web site (www.insightworld.org), mail queries, or by calling +1-972-473-5136.

NOTES